How rare is a book that you want ...
Kornfield's All I See Is Grace *is that bo*...
for Jesus" book. No. This one's for real. It is an honest, winsome, compelling account of Debbie's long, roller coaster faith journey with her daughter Karis, born with a birth defect, struggling for survival, yet full of life for all of her thirty years. No matter where you are in your own life, you will find yourself in this book and live your next day with renewed strength and yes, joy.

The Rev. Dr. Ann Paton, Professor Emerita Geneva College, beloved pastor, preacher, and teacher in the Pittsburgh diocese of the Anglican Church of North America

As I read the story shared on these pages, I felt I was on holy ground. With breath-taking authenticity, Debra invites us into her family's sacred journey with Jesus in the face of her beloved daughter Karis's unfathomable suffering. As she unfolds Karis's journal entries, Debra deftly guides us into the interior of her daughter's soul and reveals stunning beauty purified by pain. Their tender hearts touch our own and point us to the grace available in Christ as we pass through life's greatest struggles.

Dr. Dean Carlson, President, One Challenge International

"Here is the world. Beautiful and terrible things will happen" wrote Frederick Buechner. "Don't be afraid. God is with you." Reading All I See is Grace *brought these words to mind as I walked again with Karis and recalled how powerfully she brought that light and grace to those around her.*

Dr. George Mazariegos, Director of Pediatric Transplantation, Children's Hospital of Pittsburgh

What a poignant and well-told story. A wonderful book that deeply honors Karis's life. For anyone who has ever suffered a chronic heartache or physical pain, or loved someone who has, Karis's story will touch and lift and comfort you. A beautifully woven mother-daughter story of surviving and thriving, balanced with the art of surrender and letting go. Sometimes the greatest miracles are those we can't touch or see. You will love this book.

Becky Johnson, co-author (with her daughter Rachel Randolph) *Nourished: A Search for Health, Happiness and a Full Night's Sleep* and *We Laugh, We Cry, We Cook* (Zondervan)

While this book will make you cry, the irrepressible joy of two extraordinary souls shines brightly. For everyone who has ever asked "Why, Lord?" here is a gentle, encouraging response grounded in God's presence and grace.

The Rt. Rev. James L. Hobby, Bishop of Pittsburgh, Anglican Church of North America

Bookstores are full of stories about how God helps in times of suffering. But this book is different. Beautifully written, this is the poignant tale of a remarkable young woman whose short life was full of astonishing turns and faith-filling experiences. I recommend this to everyone who wants a fresh look at God in the midst of struggle and heartbreak.

Dr. Gerald McDermott, Beeson Divinity School, Co-author, *Cancer: A Medical and Spiritual Guide for Patients and Their Families,* among many other published works

Once I started reading "All I see is Grace" I could not put it down. I lay awake cherishing each chapter, story, and surprising response to adversity. Karis was never able to do all she dreamed of. But those around her were marked by the pureness, beauty and joy in her life as she courageously walked through impossibly painful situations with grace, a glow on her face, and genuine concern for each person she interacted with. Karis brightened our world and inspired us to be better people. She taught us about love, and made the world a kinder, more beautiful place. She showed us how to live through difficult times and continue to confide in our all loving, powerful God. I was Karis's Elementary School principal, High School discipleship leader and a "Tia" [auntie] in our mission, but SHE was my teacher in life.

Claudia Limpic, OC International, formerly Pan American Christian Academy, São Paulo, Brazil

I want to thank you for the privilege of sharing this beautiful, well written, gracefully edited book. Attached is my reviewed copy of All I See Is Grace. I meant to do it in several sittings, but could not stop reading. Having been a Karis blog reader for many of the years mentioned, it was a gift to read a fuller story, Karis's story.

Deanna Van Elswyk, Executive Assistant to the President, Evangelical College; long-time missions supporter

I found this story very moving. Debra implicitly raised a lot of important ethical questions even when she didn't directly address them. For example, I kept thinking that both she and Karis were trying to do and be a whole lot more than was humanly possible or even desirable. I know that the missionary spirit is sacrificial, and I applaud that: most of us spoiled Americans need a good dose of self-sacrifice. At the same time, why must others always come first? When does a dying person or an overwhelmed caregiver realize that her own needs are just as important as other people's? How do we even make decisions we can live with? Such questions are universal, but the answers are intensely personal. I am thankful for the opportunity to walk with Debra and Karis on their agonizing but love-filled journey.

LaVonne Neff livelydust.blogspot.com, retired editor at IVP and Loyola Press (among others)

Debra Kornfield preaches the gospel of Jesus Christ crucified from the vantage point of her own personal Calvary. Taking us through scientifically inexplicable miracles and crushing setbacks, this story is a must read for Christians, atheists and all of us who rarely get to see faith reverse the absurdity of suffering so gracefully and joyfully as in the life of Karis.

Dr. Georges Montillet, author and speaker, Near Eastern Languages and Civilizations

To know Karis was to be loved by her. For those of us who had the opportunity to be welcomed in by her clear blue eyes, it wasn't her sickness, but her hunger to live and to love, and to love each of us personally, that marked us. As someone who needed her forgiveness, little did I realize just how strong that love was. The life of it warms these pages, the touch of the young woman I had known, and who I discovered in new ways as I read. Excerpts from her personal journals reveal how her struggle with fatal chronic illness from the moment of her birth was just one part of her larger, constant dialogue with God: messy, raw, and beautiful in its honesty. This book, like Karis's life, offers no clean, comfortable answers. But for those willing to walk alongside her through these pages, may it be a door to know Karis and to be touched by the love she carried.

Anthony

Karis

ALL I SEE IS GRACE

Alex and
Jane,
wishing you
deep joy
even in the
tough times
& Debbie
2 Co 4:16-17

Debra Kornfield

*with selections from the journals
and poetry of Karis Joy Kornfield*

WESTBOW
P R E S S®
A DIVISION OF THOMAS NELSON
& ZONDERVAN

WestBow Press books may be ordered through booksellers or by contacting:

WestBow Press
A Division of Thomas Nelson & Zondervan
1663 Liberty Drive
Bloomington, IN 47403
www.westbowpress.com
1 (866) 928-1240

ISBN: 978-1-9736-3091-3 (sc)
ISBN: 978-1-9736-3092-0 (hc)
ISBN: 978-1-9736-3090-6 (e)

Library of Congress Control Number: 2018907003

Print information available on the last page.

WestBow Press rev. date: 7/3/2018

This book is dedicated with love

To my beloved, David
You believed in this book against all odds.
And to our precious children: Daniel, Rachel, and Valerie
You walked this journey with us from beginning to end.

And to Dr. George Mazariegos
*representing the tough, resilient, compassionate
intestinal transplant professionals and families of Pittsburgh
at both Children's Hospital and Montefiore.*

And to
Our far-flung extended family
Karis's godparents, Peter and Sharon Taylor
Servants of Christ, Port Huron, MI
OC International
Sepal Brasil
Pan American Christian Academy
Our neighbors on Rua El Ferrol
Dr. Carlos Garcia
Primeira Igreja Batista em Jardim das Imbuias, São Paulo
The University of Notre Dame
Dr. James and Barbara Blechl
Church of the Ascension, Pittsburgh
Jonah's Call, Pittsburgh
The IMT
Karis's Beloveds (likely including *you*)
By turns, you cocooned our family until Karis was ready to fly.

And to Anthony
Hoping this book will return to you even more than you put into it.

And to the Body of Christ worldwide
Karis interceded for you. I believe she still does.

Contents

Three Stories Intertwined

At 24, Karis wrote, *"May they say this of me when they say nothing else, when I am gone: she loved me. God loved me through her"* (September 23, 2007).

The flood of reminiscences from around the world after Karis Joy Kornfield died at age 30 on February 5, 2014 testified to this legacy. Each person felt specially loved by her; many said they first understood God's love through experiencing hers. Karis's passion for people of all types and stripes soaks through the pages of her journals as she intercedes for her "Beloveds," as she called her friends and family. If she knew you, she prayed for you!

All I See is Grace relates the joy-filled, intrepid way Karis lived and loved despite severe, chronic intestinal illness. This is the first strand: the Karis all of us could see and know. But Karis's journals revealed to me a person we didn't see or know, one who was truly known only to her heavenly Father. This second strand pulls in another person's life, integral to hers, her "Amado," her beloved—at first only in her romantic imagination, but later as solid and real and improbable as her confidence in God against all odds. This narrative took me completely by surprise as I read Karis's journals, dramatically changing my understanding of how she would tell her story.

If you knew Karis, you have your own perspective, and would surely tell her story differently than I. But the third intertwining is inevitably my own story, as for thirty years I rode Karis's roller coaster with her. Karis and I were of necessity thrown together more than most mothers and their daughters. This was both privilege and pressure, for what young woman wants to be dependent, and what mother wants to watch her child suffer?

In her notebooks Karis rarely provided context, such mundane details as place and time and events of the day. I've done my best to fill in that part. Instead, her journals consist largely of transparent conversations with her Papa God, her Father. Through her journals we begin to comprehend what anchored Karis. We see both the struggles and the strength behind her smile. We watch her wrestle in raw anguish over her losses. And through her eyes we see compelling visions of God the Father who as with Jesus in Gethsemane heard and answered even when the physical suffering did not change (Hebrews 5:7).

About half of Karis's journaling was intercession. To protect the privacy of these Beloveds, I have laid aside those pages. I have drawn, though, from the other half of Karis's writing: why she stubbornly believed God was worthy of her trust, despite the perplexity, frustration, and even outrage she freely expressed as her roller coaster twisted and turned.

As can be expected of journal writing, Karis's first concern was not with syntax, grammar, spelling, or proper punctuation. So if you see something you want to "correct" in her journal excerpts, relax. Remember that it's a journal, not polished, formal writing. Karis journaled in five languages. For simplicity, I decided not to identify every time that what I cite is actually a translation.

This story is by turns funny, surprising, challenging, and comforting. But it is not clean and tidy. Karis was born with intestines that did not function. Her reality was disarrayed daily by the messy results. I have tried to write as tastefully as possible, but if I completely sanitize this dimension of her life, I won't have told *her* story. If you have difficulty reading this, imagine *living* it.

Like many of us, I tend to like comfort, easy solutions, health, wealth, and happiness. Karis left for us instead a treasure of trust, feisty determination, and joy distinctively forged through living faithfully one day at a time. At age 18 (Nov 2001) Karis wrote, *"I'm crying because I'm afraid I'll never write anything worth publishing, nothing that will reach out and Touch—and that fear hurts worse than death."* She was not able to write the novels, volumes of poetry and insightful academic essays she dreamed about. But through her journals she does "reach out and Touch" our own essential struggles.

Karis's story represents many others who have suffered more than their "fair" share, whether physically or in other ways. Over the course of her life she and I were privileged to know so many within and outside of the transplant community who faced daunting circumstances with grace and courage, who by their faith, humor, tenacity, resilience, and achievements encouraged and nurtured us. This book is for you, Beloveds, with all my love and Karis's. If you have suffered or have walked closely with someone who has, this book honors you.

To protect the identity of some people in this story, I have changed their names. Others preferred I use their true names. Medical personnel and others in professional roles are identified simply with an initial. Please don't try to sort out who is who; you might guess wrong. Please, just enjoy the story.

I think Karis and I and our family—my husband Dave, our son Dan and younger daughters Rachel and Valerie—owe more to more people than anyone else in the history of the world. Saying "thank you" seems totally inadequate, but for many of you who knew and loved Karis, prayed and cared for her, it's the best I can do. As you read, *please write yourself into the story*. You know where you belong and what you did for her and for me and for us. You have many memories of her that don't fit within the scope of this book. Please know that I, and Karis, and our family, are deeply grateful. We know we would not have survived without you. As we say in Brazil, "May God reward you."

Prologue

The week after Karis died, I attacked my house. I could no longer tolerate all the medical stuff which had held my daughter captive. For days I frenetically gathered, hauled, sorted, sold, returned, threw away or gave away her hospital bed, wheelchair, IV pole, oxygen concentrator, medications, lab reports and heaps of other paraphernalia. I stripped away everything which said, "Severe chronic illness here."

Then, suddenly spent, I collapsed on the couch where Karis had "lived" for most of her last years. I looked around at my clean, orderly, ordinary house, and burst into tears. There were no more medical artifacts to remind me of Karis's suffering. But there was also no Karis.

I couldn't take it in. I couldn't believe it was actually true.

After that outburst, I didn't cry again for many weeks. I went through the motions of doing what needed to be done, responding (apparently) to the people who crossed my path, taping on our living room wall the dozens of condolence cards the mailman delivered each day.

Still, I didn't believe Karis was actually gone. I did believe her *illness* was over. I didn't expect to see the *sick* Karis again. Yet I anticipated hearing our front door open, savoring her light step and cheery greeting and feeling her warm hug. I expected to be regaled with tales of people she had met and her plans for the evening and what exotic food she wanted to make for dinner. I could hear her laughter and almost catch her impish smile and the blue sparkling of her eyes as she planned a surprise for her sisters.

I didn't mention this to anyone. I nodded graciously as people told me she was better off in Heaven. Inside though, I waited. Years later, I still wait. It feels impossible that someone so vibrant, so *alive,* could be dead. Yes, I *know:* she's alive in Heaven. But…

Over and over I re-played the YouTube of Karis's memorial service, to make myself believe she was gone. I listened to the twenty-two pieces of music as I went about my housework. I recalled the words people said about Karis, even the words I said myself. I gazed at video images of the friends who came through icy winter conditions to tell us how important Karis had been to them. I looked at the cards, read the e-mails, printed out many lovely tributes. I imagined Karis dancing in Heaven. I asked God to give her hugs for me. *But….*

My heart waited because it wasn't right, fair, or possible that we would live the rest of our lives here on Earth without her. God could not take Karis out of her messed-up frame but not give her back to *us* well and strong again.

After a long time, I started looking through Karis's personal stuff, mentally apologizing for invading her privacy. Karis was a packrat. I found hundreds of cards and letters received from friends during her ten years in and out of hospitals in Pittsburgh. I found stories and poems, half-written letters, keepsakes from concerts, plays and parties. I found notebooks stuffed with Notre Dame class notes, decorated with calligraphy and interspersed with musings, prayers, and poems apparently dashed off in the midst of chemistry lectures, Arabic conjugations, and discourses in philosophy and theology, sub-Saharan history, economics, politics, anthropology and human rights.

Scattered through all of this I found journals. I started collecting these in a box, marking dates on their covers and putting them into chronological order. But I couldn't read them. Karis would be devastated when she walked through the front door of our house to find I had so disrespected her privacy.

Months later, I finally picked up the journal she wrote at age nine. . . To my surprise and sometimes consternation as over the ensuing months I read thousands of closely-written pages, I discovered a daughter I had not fully known, even while living alongside her for most of her thirty years. I read about a rich intimacy with God I had seen only in glimpses, marked by such trust that Karis could communicate transparently with her heavenly Father intense struggles, questions, and profound losses. Often I felt envious. Why had Karis not trusted *me* enough to share so with me?

For example, while in high school in São Paulo, Brazil, when she was well enough, Karis would appear for breakfast with a cheery greeting and a smile on her face. Until I read her journals I had no idea that she might have spent much of the previous night awake, wrestling with God, pouring out to him her anguished doubts and even despair; finding, finally, in the early hours, the strength and confidence she needed in order to live another day.

All I saw was the smile on her face as she came down the stairs ready for school.

The victories Karis achieved through those intimate, teary, often nocturnal encounters with God are what made possible the joyful, radiant, quirky, compassionate Karis who touched all of us who knew her. I found in Karis's journals responses not to my "why" questions—*Why* did my little girl have to suffer so much, for so long?—but rather to a "how" question: *How* in the face of that suffering did she maintain and nurture trust, joy, love, and hope?

Reading Karis's journals was an intensely emotional journey. I could read only small bits at a time. Over those weeks and months I was flooded with memories I had to re-visit—and in many cases re-frame—because of what Karis revealed about herself in that ragtag collection of notebooks.

I learned that Karis experienced a life-altering event when she was 16. Teenage friends prayed over her a promise and a prophecy, which resonated with her as personal words from God. She latched on to these words and shaped her inner world around them, believing she would not die before this promise and prophecy were fulfilled. But she didn't share any of this with her father and me.

Curious, I read on. Sure enough, as events unfolded, the promise and the prophecy *were* the framework through which Karis viewed her life. Over time, though, her circumstances did not foster hope of fulfilling either one. Was their importance to Karis simply a product of her own imagination, rather than a true word from God? I was prepared to accept their significance *to her*, but I was skeptical that they reflected true divine purpose.

I was skeptical until . . . Oh, but I'm getting so ahead of the story. Here we go, then. Climb aboard and ride Karis's roller coaster with me.

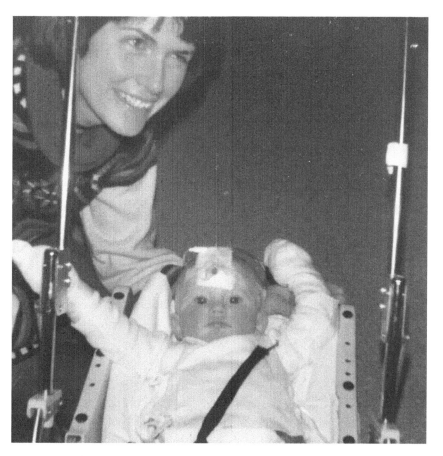

While Karis had an IV in the middle of her forehead,
we called her "The Coalminer."

CHAPTER 1

Choose Life

Birth to Six Weeks
May 5-June 17, 1983
Wheaton and Chicago

Dr. R, chief of pediatric surgery at the children's hospital in Chicago, was notably absent from the team of doctors who met with Dave and me one Friday morning to tell us Karis's condition was incompatible with life. They said we should disconnect Karis from medical support, sedate her, and let her die.

That evening, Dave and I tried to focus on lovely music at the symphony, a gift from friends who thought we needed a break from the hospital. But I couldn't stop the tears. At intermission, we gave up. David took me to a nearby park and tried to comfort me, but his words about God's sovereignty only frustrated and angered me. I asked him for some time alone and wandered off, hardly noticing the beauty of the warm June evening.

"If you're a God of love," I railed through my tears, "how can you allow little ones to suffer? Not just Karis but every one of the children in that hospital! If you don't care enough or aren't powerful enough to heal the children, why should I follow you? Why should I trust you?"

Utterly spent, I threw myself down on the grass. Every time I tried to stop crying, a vision of my baby daughter's violated little body intruded: a tube protruding from her nose, another plastic tube coiled on her chest above an ugly red scar that bisected her abdomen, with a strawberry-like ostomy[1] perched nearby.

Finally, as my weeping calmed, I heard someone speaking to me. I sat up and looked around to see who was there. "I will never leave you nor forsake you," said the voice. "But if you turn away from me, you will not know my presence with you."

God had spoken to me—*out loud!* I sat trembling on the grass, engulfed by emotions. I knew he was still there, waiting for me to decide. I had no

---

[1] At five weeks Karis's small bowel had been cut and the end brought out through her abdomen. This attempt to help a bowel to function is called an ileostomy.

bargaining power. I had only to choose: trust or turn away. Trust him without understanding, without any promises except his presence with me, or reject him and allow bitterness to begin digging a hole into my heart.

If I turned away from God, my six-week-old daughter would still die. I would be left without her *and* without God, whom I had known and loved all my life.

Still he waited.

"Lord," I finally said, "I want to trust you. I do. But this hurts so badly that I know I will need a lot of help. Please, please help me."

I lay back in the grass-turned-holy ground. A different series of images flashed through my mind. Each one showed me how God had been present with us the past six weeks. He knew. He cared. He had not abandoned us. I recalled the loveliness of my newborn, her chubbiness sustaining her through the days without nutrition following her birth. I remembered the ease of her delivery and my mother's timely arrival in the United States from Guatemala, exactly when we needed her, as I fought post-partum infection.

I recalled my father first meeting Karis at eleven days and ordering us to the doctor. I chuckled at the memory of Dr. W with bright-yellow milk running down his face from Karis's bilious vomiting, shouting orders into the telephone. It was harder to be grateful for sardonic Dr. R, yet God had used him to keep Karis alive and to figure out why her intestine didn't work: she had only 20 percent of the normal number of nerves, and those were small and malformed. "Impossible for this intestine ever to function . . ." Dr. R said.

Still in God's palpable presence, I thought about the prayer vigil our church had planned for Karis at the hospital the next evening—the very weekend we were supposed to think about ending her life. I thought gratefully of the doctors' agreement to give us until Monday to make our decision.

As a light summer breeze dried my tears, my conviction solidified: we should *not* take action to end Karis's life. God who was *there*, literally right there, surrounding me, gave me courage to trust him in this. I was a nurse. I could learn to administer TPN[2] and care for a central line. I would ask to take Karis home, a radical idea in 1983 when TPN for infants was brand new.

I let my mind play over Karis's spunkiness and feistiness, her charm, and her trust in us—her joy and smiles that had already knit her tightly into our hearts. I began imagining our family together again, restoring stability to our twenty-two-month-old Danny who overnight had gained a sister and lost his mother as I spent every possible minute with Karis at the hospital.

Gradually, as grass tickled my cheek, I began to feel peace. God's astounding presence was enough. It was enough to go home with my husband and let myself sleep. Enough to leave perplexities and contradictions and grief and tomorrow's worries to tomorrow. Enough.

---

[2] Though commonly used today, in 1983, TPN (total parenteral nutrition) was still experimental. It is nutrition infused directly into the blood stream through a central IV line into the heart to be dispersed quickly through the body, completely bypassing the digestive system.

One-year-old Karis trying to keep up with her big brother Danny

CHAPTER 2

Roller Coaster

Six Weeks to Two and a Half Years
June 18, 1983-December, 1985
Wheaton and Port Huron

Twenty-four hours after my encounter with God in the park, our church gathered at the hospital to pray over Karis Joy. Everyone agreed we should *choose life*. They told us God had a purpose for this little one —not just for our family but for the Body of Christ worldwide! Danny's godmother, our friend Jan, had a vision of Karis well at three years old, riding a tricycle down a sunny sidewalk in front of a gray house, her blonde braids bouncing.

That night, unaccountably, Karis's intestine started working! The doctors' basic premise—*this intestine can never function*—was foiled by the mundanity of a soiled ostomy pouch. Monday morning, Dr. R, against the judgment of his team, agreed to let us take Karis home.

Clearly, through the prayers of his people, God had healed our baby's intestinal nerves! Our friend Jan's vision of Karis healed at three? That must have been her imagination, because Karis thrived. Dave and I mentally and emotionally closed the chapter of her first two confusing months and looked forward to a delightful future with our darling Danny and our precious, winsome little girl.

But six months later, on New Year's Eve, our happy world fell apart. Karis started vomiting again, as she had in her first weeks of life. We greeted 1984 back in the hospital, confused and frightened. Dr. R's scoffing rang in my ears. *"What did you think—that God performed a miracle?"*

Actually, yes! God *had* performed a miracle! For six months, Karis's intestine had functioned *normally*. The doctors had told us this was impossible, so God *must* have healed her!

How then could she be so sick once again?

Over the next two years, we rode a roller coaster that screeched and plunged with no warning and no apparent destination. Karis was hospitalized twenty-two times, sometimes for several weeks at a time. She had more surgeries, each one removing additional pieces of her small bowel, supported by periods back on TPN. Several times the doctors thought Karis wouldn't survive. God gave her back to us each time, but the nurses stopped calling Karis "Miracle Baby." Dave and I were bruised and baffled.

These years were very challenging for us as a family. Dave traveled frequently for work and I was focused on keeping Karis alive. Danny could not safely be at the hospital and had to be taken care of by our friends.

If we could do it over, we would find a way to be more present for each other as a whole family unit, rather than pulled in so many directions, each with a greater load than we could individually bear. Dave and I both came from missionary families where ministry objectives came first. Caring for the family was often more about meeting physical needs than emotional needs. Through a lifetime of learning we have altered those values, but we were not there yet.

Surprisingly, Karis's emerging personality helped energize us. Between crises, Karis *loved* life. She never exhibited stranger anxiety. Her easy trust in people was a gift that made no sense given all the physical distress and painful interventions she suffered. Yet she always came back smiling, endearing herself to all who knew her. She made up for her times in the hospital with extra energy to invest in life at home.

To Dr. R's annoyance, I refused to treat Karis like an invalid. Endless testing had shown her to be perfectly normal, with only one little problem: inadequate innervation of her intestines, which I determined should *not* define her.

Every time Karis was in crisis though, Dr. R dumped his frustration on me. He ordered me to stop taking risks like going camping, swimming, or sledding—all the things Karis loved and Danny needed. These activities were life-giving, I insisted. They did *not* make Karis's condition worse. As she had energy, Karis engaged in all the fun, mischief, play, and learning available. She had an impish sense of humor and a wonderful grin. She lived with zest, loved people, and assumed everyone—including Dr. R— loved her.

On April 19, 1985, we celebrated the birth of a precious new daughter, who was born perfectly normal. My relief, gratitude, and delight were enormous. We named her Rachel ("little lamb") Dawn because she was an Easter baby. Rachel did everything babies are supposed to do, right on schedule. We joked that she was the model for developmental textbooks.

To my sorrow, I had to wean Rachel early due to Karis's frequent hospitalizations. It wasn't safe for baby Rachel to be at the hospital surrounded by sick children, so she quickly became a Daddy's girl. Sweet Rachel increased our incentive to keep Karis at home every day we possibly could, resorting to hospital care only when we absolutely did not have adequate resources at home. Dr. R regularly contested my judgment on this. He would have preferred that Karis live at the hospital.

In December 1985, when Rachel was eight months old, Karis was two, and Danny was four, we moved from Wheaton to Port Huron, Michigan, transferring Karis's medical care to Dr. P, a surgeon at the children's hospital in Detroit, an hour south of Port Huron. *Oh God, thank you, thank you, thank you for using Dr. P to heal my bruised heart! Thank you for taking us to Port Huron so Karis* and I *could be cared for by such a kind and able man.*

I have often pondered my experience with Karis when she was little, spending so much time in clinic treatment rooms and hospital recovery rooms. As a toddler, she frequently had to undergo frightening and painful medical procedures. I watched many other young children suffer similar ordeals, screaming and angry, striking out at their parents and nurses. Sometimes they had to be physically restrained in order to receive the treatments they needed but could not possibly understand.

Karis responded differently. She pulled close to me, letting my strength support her through the pain.

I realize I have a similar choice when faced with circumstances that I, like a two-year-old, cannot understand. I can fight my Father, or I can pull close and let *his* strength carry me through.

Karis, baby Valerie, and Rachel playing in our back yard in Port Huron.

CHAPTER 3

Visions and Dreams

Two-and-a-Half to Seven Years
January 1986-June 1990
Port Huron, Detroit, and Brazil!

When she was in eighth grade, Karis wrote:

Though I was sick for most of my first three years, by some miracle my earliest memories fail to capture the pain. I remember a colorful waiting room, the Ronald McDonald House, Mommy's beautiful smile, Daddy's strong arms, songs we sang and games we played. Since I've been old enough to consciously remember anything, I haven't concentrated on the pain. I remember distinctly noticing, not when it hurt, but when it didn't hurt. And when it did, I would sing or suck my thumb, trying to ignore the pain.

Through 1986 as we adjusted to life in Port Huron, Karis's good times became rarer, and were finally swallowed up in chronic distress. By the time she was three, Karis brought to mind photos of starving children with their swollen tummies and spindly arms and legs, a defeated look in her eyes. Karis had no energy and spent most of her time lying on our couch sucking her thumb, with occasional tears rolling down her cheeks. Diarrhea poured out of her little body like water.

Dr. P discussed Karis's case with other specialists, including Dr. R, but no one knew what to do for her. Finally, in the fall of 1986, Dr. P told us he wanted to try another surgery to remove yet one more section of her intestine and create a new ileostomy. He could not promise this would help her, but it was the only idea he had, and she wouldn't survive much longer the way she was.

I rejected Dr. P's proposal. *Put my suffering little girl through another major surgery just because the doctor can't think of anything else to do? With no clear picture of how or whether it might help her? Not on my watch, thank you very much!*

Dave, however, longed to do *something* for her. We took our dilemma to our church and asked them to pray with us for direction. The following Sunday, they told us unanimously that we should go ahead with the surgery. Grudgingly, I submitted. Karis was hospitalized for a few weeks on TPN to build her strength for better surviving the surgery, which took place in early December.

Watching Karis over the next few months was one of the most amazing experiences of my life. She bounced back from surgery so fast we were able to take her home from the hospital in time for Christmas. She started eating all kinds of real food, and growing so quickly I could hardly keep her in clothes that fit. Within four months she grew four inches and gained ten pounds! She was back on the growth chart.

Karis's energy returned. Soon she was running around and playing with Danny and Rachel, conquering developmental milestones in which she had lagged. It was like watching a wilted little flower blossom in a spring rain. Almost every day, Karis ran to find me and exclaimed, "Mommy, nothing hurts!"

One beautiful spring morning near the end of April 1987, I looked out the window above the kitchen sink and saw five-year-old Danny teaching Karis to ride his old tricycle. I had a strange sense of *déjà vu*. Suddenly our friend Jan's vision flashed into my mind, from so long ago it felt like a different lifetime. But there it was: Karis pedaling a tricycle down the sunny sidewalk in front of our new gray house, her blonde braids bouncing on her shoulders. I broke out in goose bumps. Tears flowed by the time I reached the phone to call Dave. Jan had envisioned Karis healed at age three, and her fourth birthday was still a week away.

"David," I said into the phone. "Karis is well! We can move to Brazil!"

On his first trip to Brazil two years before, Dave was convinced God was calling us there. He had kept this dream alive by traveling to Brazil several more times. When I realized that God had fulfilled Jan's vision, I believed Dave's dream could also come true! We began researching mission boards, and a few months later, joined OC International.

On January 18, 1988, two weeks after we joined OC, our last child, Valerie Michelle, was born whole and healthy. Four-year-old Karis adored her darling baby sister, a "living dolly" who moved, laughed, cried, and could be dressed up to fit any role her older sisters needed for their imaginative play.

Our family refocused: from constant concern for Karis's health, we shifted to preparations for moving to Brazil! The summer of 1988, our whole family attended ten weeks of missionary training in California. We delighted in the wonders of Yosemite and celebrated Danny's seventh birthday with a ride on a San Francisco cable car. In August, we returned to Port Huron for another couple of years while we pursued Brazilian visas, finances, and prayer support for our missionary work. After the births of three sisters, Danny decided we were going to Brazil to find a brother for him.

One afternoon Karis and her kindergarten classmates were playing outside for recess when Karis's ileostomy pouch came completely off, causing a huge, odorous mess. Karis was very quiet as we cleaned her up at home, and I imagined she must be struggling with shame and embarrassment. When she finally spoke, though, her take on the situation surprised me.

"Mom, when we go back to school tomorrow could you come with me? I'm feeling sad for the kids. I saw their faces and I don't think they understand about me. It's not fair for them. They should have the chance to know how God saved my life and I think you could explain it to them better than I can cuz I was just a baby when I got this ileostomy. They should know God loves me and he loves them too."

A year later, six-year-old Karis stomped into the house and slammed the door, her face a thundercloud.

"Honey, what's wrong? Did something happen at school?" I asked in alarm.

"Mom, it's not fair! The English language is ridiculous! Who came up with the stupid idea of making O-U-G-H sound so many different ways? I counted five today and maybe there are even more!"

"But sweetheart, why is this upsetting you so much?"

"Oh Mom, can't you see? It's OK for me because I already know how to read. But don't you see how hard it is for the kids who are just learning? Why make something that's already hard for them even harder, for no reason? And my teacher says I may NOT re-invent the spelling of the English language! I'm so mad I'm going to walk around the block!"

In June of 1990, Dave's dream from 1984 finally came true! Karis had just turned seven, Danny was almost nine, curly-haired Rachel five, and little Valerie two. Our new mission team, Sepal Brasil, met us at the airport in São Paulo, and our great Brazilian adventure began!

For the next two years, an important time for adjusting to our brand-new life in the São Paulo megalopolis, Karis continued to enjoy good health. We began learning Portuguese, and enrolled Danny (fourth grade), Karis (second grade), and Rachel (kindergarten) in their new school, Pan American Christian Academy (PACA). We found an apartment, and a year later, a house near school.

Karis embraced Brazil with typical enthusiasm, and soon corrected my Portuguese, preferred Brazilian food, discussed with her brother the merits of various São Paulo soccer teams, called our city "Sampa" and herself a "Paulista," and collected a new set of friends. Occasionally, when I watched Karis run out to play with neighbor kids in the street by our house, I thought, "If only Dr. R could see you now!" God's vision for our little girl's life, even at age seven, was greater than any of us could have imagined.

Karis began to find her voice, in journaling and in poetry.

CHAPTER 4

Every Good Day is a Miracle

Ages Nine to Twelve
January 1993-June 1995
São Paulo, Brazil

Returning to São Paulo in January, 1993 from a Kornfield Christmas family reunion in Bolivia, I realized I was happy to be back! God was answering my prayer that I would *enjoy* living in a mega-city, not just tolerate it. At the same time, concern flickered at the back of my mind. During our three weeks away, Karis had started throwing up again. Bolivian food and water could not explain *bilious* vomiting and the degree of distention and tummy pain nine-year-old Karis was grappling with once again. Dave's brother Bill was the first to discover Karis throwing up, in the middle of the night, trying not to disturb anyone.

I reminded God that I had entrusted Karis to his care when we began our missionary adventure. For five years he had kept her well, so he could certainly keep on doing it! Nevertheless, over the next year and a half Karis's symptoms gradually worsened. Karis wrote (Mar 19, 1993), *"I am very, very tired. Last night I was very sick. I didn't eat a snack or supper or anything."*

Increasingly, Karis's tummy-illness interfered with favorite activities: playing guitar, helping lead the neighborhood children's club in our home, basketball, jogging, playing dress-up with kids from our street, reading voraciously, writing poetry, swimming, dancing, drawing, all kinds of crafts, and teaching her sisters whatever she learned. Still, she wrote in her first journal (age nine), *"Every bit of sadness is much smaller than my gladness."* Consistent with her middle name, she seemed to have an endless supply of joy.

We spent June and July 1994 in the United States visiting family, friends, and supporters, our first time back since we had flown to Brazil four years before. But Karis was sick. Halfway through our time in the United States,

Dr. P proposed a surgery to remove adhesions.[3] He took advantage of the several-hour surgery to biopsy Karis's intestine and stomach. To our astonishment, *these biopsies were identical to those done when Karis was five weeks old!* She still had very few, small, scattered, and malformed intestinal nerves. We were left with huge questions:

What then had God done the night of the prayer meeting at the hospital in Chicago when Karis's intestine began functioning for the first time—and continued to function for *six months*?!

What had God done through the surgery when she was three that initiated a five-year period of good health following the fulfillment of Jan's vision?

Dr. P had no answers. He agreed with Dr. R's conclusion when Karis was an infant: *Physiologically, there was no possibility her intestine could function.* Instead of being frustrated when Karis was sick, we should be amazed whenever her intestine worked. In other words . . . **each day of those good years had been a miracle!**

Post-surgery, Karis participated as she could in the events of our last weeks in the United States, but frequently required crash times to recover energy, and seemed to be tummy-sick as often as before.

On the plane back to Brazil, when the flight attendant announced our descent into São Paulo, Rachel stood up on her seat and started chanting, "Brasil! Brasil! Brasil!" The cry spread until it seemed everyone in the plane was chanting as we landed. We were SOOOO happy to be home.

That fall (spring in Brazil), Karis (age eleven) recorded a series of

---

[3] Abdominal adhesions are bands of fibrous tissue which often form after abdominal surgeries, causing organs and tissues to stick or bind together instead of sliding past each other as the body moves. Adhesions can become larger and tighter as time passes. They cannot be detected by tests nor seen by imaging techniques. They are most often identified through exploratory surgery performed because of otherwise unexplained symptoms.

observations from her studies of Jesus healing people in the book of Mark. In a Thanksgiving meditation, she wrote, *"God is a friend who understands me. With Him, I am a conqueror in my sufferings. I can develop perseverance, character, hope, and finally, joy. God is my joy and joy is my strength. I can win in losing. I am thankful my childhood has been full and happy, and that I could grow up with Jesus at my side."*

One Saturday morning as Dave and I dawdled over breakfast, Karis walked into the kitchen looking very serious. "Mom and Dad, I don't want you to pray any more for me to be healed. I read 2 Corinthians 12 this morning. Paul prayed three times for God to heal him and God said no. *Thousands* of prayers have been said for me and God can heal me if he wants to, but it seems like he has said no. I want you to pray instead that God will be glorified through my life whether I'm well or not. I just memorized 2 Corinthians 12:9, '**My grace is sufficient for you, for my power is made perfect in weakness**.' That's going to be my life verse from now on."

"Honey, we can't stop other people from praying, and we won't stop seeking medical help for you," her dad replied. "But Mom and I can pray as you are requesting. Let's see what God does."

We enjoyed a visit from cousins Claire (age nine), Sarah (eight), and their parents for Christmas 1994. The kids all got sunburned swimming in the PACA pool on Christmas Eve. Karis (eleven), Rachel (nine), and Valerie (six) choreographed and performed dances to the "Hallelujah Chorus" and Simon and Garfunkel's "Patterns" as their Christmas gift for their father.

After Christmas, I took Karis to Detroit, where in January, 1995 Dr. P operated again, removing another section of her malfunctioning intestine. Dr. P told us we might hear rumors about intestinal transplantation, but to pay no attention. He didn't believe it would ever be successful.

For the first time, we heard Dr. P call Karis's condition Chronic Intestinal

Pseudo-Obstruction Syndrome (CIPS; now called CIP or CIPO).[4] Thanks to TPN, a few babies with symptoms like Karis's were now living long enough to be diagnosed with CIPO. Karis's type, congenital primary neuropathic hypoganglionic CIPO, is extremely rare and is still considered incompatible with life apart from successful intestinal transplant. As far as we know, Karis was the first person in the world to survive infancy with this diagnosis.[5]

At her one-month post-surgery check-up, Dr. P cleared Karis for return to Brazil. For a while, her health improved! I felt I could begin a graduate program in family counseling, offered Friday evenings and Saturdays at a local seminary. As I could, I worked away at those courses for the next several years. Studying in Portuguese expanded my mastery of the language and of a Brazilian world view. Using public transportation to cross our mega-city was an adventure. I loved the practicality of what I was learning and it was rewarding to feel I could better understand and help others.

After this surgery, as she did whenever she was in a "good" period of health, Karis engaged the world with gusto. She experienced a belated growth spurt, began jogging with Dave and Danny and participating in school athletics, excelled at academics, and built deep relationships with friends at school, church, and in our neighborhood. She was deeply loyal to her classmates, even though they were entering the phase of early teen behavior that ranged from silly to atrocious. When one of her classmates was expelled for drug dealing (a significant scandal at our Christian missionary school), she was extremely sad and wondered if there wasn't some way to integrate him back into the class.

---

[4] The term "pseudo-obstruction" was invented to describe a bowel that is blocked not by a twist or other abnormality visible on an x-ray, but rather because the intestine has no motility (squeezing action), so nothing moves through it. CIPO is now used to describe a variety of conditions in which pseudo-obstruction occurs.

[5] To understand more about CIPS (CIPO), the following 2012 article may be helpful: https://rarediseases.org/rare-diseases/chronic-intestinal-pseudo-obstruction/.

One day in a father-daughter conversation, Dave asked Karis, "If you could be anyone in the whole world and through time, who would you like to be?" He imagined Karis choosing one of her beloved Brazilian worship artists, Mother Teresa, Mary the mother of Jesus . . .

Karis thought for a while and said, "Dad, I'd just like to be me."

Surprised, he asked, "Even with your ileostomy?" Now pre-adolescent, Karis had become more self-conscious. Dave knew she was embarrassed when her ileostomy leaked in public. Karis thought a little more and said, "Yes. Without this ileostomy, I wouldn't remember every day how God has healed me."

Karis wrote in her journal:

> **Oct 28, 1995** *Seal my lips and life for You. You are my Lord. I am your servant. Wet clay, ready to be formed into the potter's pot. Make me useful, Lord, like St. Francis. Love, Karis*

For almost two years following the January 1995 surgery, her middle school years, Karis enjoyed a reprieve. Dr. P's words echoed in our hearts: ***"Every good day is a miracle!"***

Karis carried by her hero, her big brother Danny

CHAPTER 5

Life Is Not Fair

Ages Fourteen to Sixteen
February 1998-November 1999
Tenth and Eleventh Grades at PACA

During Karis's high school years, her health once again declined. While her girlfriends were occupied with fashion, boys, sports, and parties, Karis often spent sleepless nights battling pain that sucked her energy like the bottom-feeders in her aquarium. I've pulled some selections from her journals to illustrate her conversations with God during her early teen years.

Age fourteen:

> **Feb 1998** *Your joy will be my strength. Show me how to share my joy, Papa and I'll step in your footprints. But don't take big steps. My legs are short.*

> **Mar 9, 1998** *Hebrews 11:4, "By faith Abel still speaks, even though he is dead."* **Oh, Lord, isn't that one of my greatest goals?! To speak. To be heard, to have a voice in other people's lives, to STAND FOR SOMETHING, even when I'm gone.** *For people to rejoice when they think of me, to say I see God in her.* **You have promised I will fulfill a purpose** *in You.*

> **Mar 26, 1998** *I didn't write to You yesterday because I was too sick. It hurt so much that I rolled up in a ball and cried. I wasn't happy. In fact it would have been very hard to smile last night. But I was covered to the ears in the peaceful kind of joy You give me, and I felt as though I had a glimpse of heaven. It was the most beautiful time.*

> **Apr 6, 1998** *I'm frightened, worried about what's happening to me. I'm tired all the time. I feel like I'm slipping away from the real world. You have given so much to me: talents, privileges, opportunities, people who love me, experiences . . . and what am I doing about it? No one this blessed should settle for this little. You made me to LIVE, not just to SURVIVE! And what, what, what am I doing but things for my own self just to MAKE IT through every day, longing for rest that never comes.*

I know you use pain, Lord. But what is the point of it all? There has got to be a REASON you let this happen. I will try not to be impatient, but some day, could you let me know?

Age fifteen:

May 23, 1998 *Lord, I feel like an overcooked, half-eaten, day-old baked potato. Sometimes I wonder what you think about that. You're a doctor, aren't you? The doctors I have are clueless. I resent them making promises they have no right to make. Couldn't you be my doctor?*

Jun 1, 1998 *My teachers have been wonderful, reducing a lot of my homework. I know I needed this break. But . . . the truth is, I hate it. There. I've said it. It seems like I've lost everything, bit by bit. Church. Sports. Friends. And now, the only thing I could really say "I did it by myself," schoolwork. It hurts. Terribly. I know in my head that You have a reason and a plan for all this. But, oh, I used to know that in more than my head!*

Karis was well enough at the end of the year to enjoy a family vacation two thousand miles north in Manaus, which would also serve as a last big family adventure before Danny went off to college. The *real* jungle was far different from the concrete jungle of São Paulo! We hired a boat and its crew to take us on a three-day trip up the Amazon River. We slept in hammocks on deck under blazing stars, watched the cavorting of pink dolphins, and fished for our dinner (Rachel caught a piranha!). We enjoyed fascinating side trips into jungle flora and fauna, caressing a sloth, playing with monkeys, ogling a giant anaconda . . .

Swinging in our hammocks under the huge Amazonian stars one night, Karis and I talked about Psalm 139. These life-giving words were an anchor that steadied her.

> O Lord . . . you know everything about me.
> You made all the delicate, inner parts of my body
> And knit me together in my mother's womb . . .
> You saw me before I was born.

Every day of my life was recorded in your book . . .

Karis owned these words very personally. She believed the "defect" in her intestines that caused her so much suffering could be used by God to bring good to her and to others. As we swung in our hammocks, she said, "Mom, **I will live exactly as long as God wishes, not one day longer or shorter**. When he decides to take me, my medical situation will be irrelevant. So *you* need to learn to stop worrying!"

> **Mar 1999** *If I were to write my story, what would it say? It would say **Your grace is sufficient, for Your strength is made perfect in weakness**. It would say "seek first the kingdom of God." How could I ever tell my own story when all I see in it is You, Lord? You have given me so much. May my life reflect You whether I am home sick or well. May I be a testimony to Your grace. **All I see is grace.***

Age Sixteen:

> **May 12, 1999** *Oh, Lord! Sometimes I am so afraid. The doctors don't know what to do with me, and it hurts so much! I feel like I'm running on energy not my own, like I'm walking on such thin ice. Lord—is it to be like this forever? I am not strong enough to bear it.*
>
> *Sometimes, inside I am rejoicing. But it is not a smiley affair, not always. Sometimes joy can be very grave or even be there bittersweet in the midst of terrible pain.*
>
> **May 19, 1999** *What now? What can I do to glorify you in this prison of mine? So strange, my body: at the same time a part of me and my enemy.*
>
> **Jun 1, 1999** *I've been poked with needles until my arms are black and blue and red. I thought last night as they poked me again, "What must it have been like for Jesus, not to be pierced by loving nurses and these tiny sharp needles, but rather the soldiers, the nails..." I remember Christ and find not the strength not to complain but rather there is nothing to complain about.*

I found Karis one morning in front of her mirror, sobbing her heart out. "I know it shouldn't matter, but it does! I am so ugly! How can people stand to look at me? How could God do this to me?"

The first time I heard Karis say, "I am so ugly," I laughed. I couldn't help myself. The night before, as she laughed in a circle of her friends, I guarantee "You are so ugly" did not cross those young men's minds when they looked at her bright blue eyes, thick, waist-long mane of shiny blonde hair, and brilliant smile. Both guys and girls wanted to be close to Karis, to absorb her joy, her compassion, her confidence.

Karis looked at me bewildered, tears still brimming in her eyes. "Karis, I'm sorry I laughed. Tell me what you see in the mirror. Tell me why you feel ugly." In her own words:

> **June 1999** *It is impossible to be happy when I focus on myself and especially when I worry about how I look: the distended, scarred tummy, the ileostomy bag that fills so quickly . . . they don't mesh with the blusinhas* [little tops] *and tight pants everyone wears. . . . God, why can't I just care a moderate, healthy, comfortable amount and smile understanding but amused by the rest?*
>
> *Oh, isn't it exciting to know one day I'll be through all this, and free? I know You could take me now, take me Home and away from this humorous body. Or You could heal me, free me and make me strong so I wouldn't—wouldn't—be crying right now . . .*

Karis agonized in her journals over how *much* this all mattered to her. Eventually she seemed to reach an uneasy acceptance of her "vanity," which she called her "secret sin."

Ever attentive to others, many of Karis's sorrows were more outward-facing. When family vacation plans had to be cancelled because of her health, or when we celebrated holidays or birthdays in a hospital, Karis grieved. "It's not fair that the whole family has to pay the price for me being sick!" She grieved over shortchanging her brother and sisters by the attention she needed from Dave and me. She hated being "teacher's pet," with due dates flexed for her when she missed school.

Karis found most unfair her access to the best doctors and hospitals in São Paulo. One morning she told me, "I'm not going to Einstein Hospital today. It's not fair."

"What's not fair, Karis? That you're sick so often?"

"No. It's not fair I get such fancy treatment. Most of my friends have to go to Grajaú Hospital when they're sick. I want to go there today and find out what it's like."

She would not be dissuaded. So we drove past the favela (slum) and through a poor neighborhood to the ER at our closest hospital. Already the inside waiting area was crowded and the rows of outdoor seats were occupied. Under a bright early-morning sun growing hotter by the minute we took our place in line for one of those outside seats.

"Karis, this isn't working. We don't have the luxury of waiting for your turn."

Karis was determined, so with misgivings I supported her (literally) as the line inched forward toward those plastic seats. Once we reached them, I ran to the car for sunscreen and the emergency two-liter bottle we always carried, and emptied her ostomy bag. She was too weak to go by herself to the single bathroom that served all these people, and if we had gone together to stand in *that* line, we would have lost our spot in *this* one. Even a little oral rehydration fluid made her throw up.

As Karis moved seat by seat toward the refuge of the indoor waiting room, her diarrhea showed no signs of letting up. I was soaked with perspiration, but her skin was dry and had gone from red to pale—a bad sign. She had stopped interacting with the people around her, another bad sign.

"Karis . . . !"

"No, I'm OK. I can do this if all of them can," indicating the ill people all around us.

"Then I have to get you to the front of the line." Without waiting to hear that wouldn't be fair, I pushed indoors and through annoyed people to the receptionist.

"My daughter is going into shock from dehydration. Her diarrhea won't stop. She needs attention now," I insisted to the impassive woman on the other side of the barrier.

"Is she bleeding?" the woman asked me. "No? Then she'll just have to wait her turn."

Elbowing back outside, I found Karis slumped against the shoulder of the man beside her, eyes closed, hands limp in her lap. "I don't think she's feeling very well," he apologized. Just then a crowd swarmed out of the ER, sweeping up the outsiders on their way to the street.

"Probably the doctor has left," the man observed. I ran back inside to confirm the story. Indeed, there would be no more ER at Grajaú until the next day.

Our benefactor helped me carry Karis to the car, and I raced across the city to Einstein Hospital. Within a few minutes, life-saving IV rehydration began. As I watched my unconscious daughter breathe, trying to process my emotions, the ER doctor appeared, brandishing a paper with her blood test results.

"Why did you wait so long to bring her in?! You have too much experience not to know she's in serious trouble this time. We have to admit her. YOU are going to be the one to explain this to Dr. G, and I don't want to be around when you do!" He listened aghast to my tale of the last several hours, and walked out shaking his head.

I repeated my story to Dr. G when he came to see Karis, now partially restored, in her hospital room.

"Sweet one, let's talk," he said, pulling up a chair beside Karis's bed. After long discussion of the injustices in Brazil, they came to an agreement. Dr. G also practiced at the public São Paulo Hospital, where there was a separate wing for people with insurance. SPH wasn't fancy like Einstein, so when she was a patient at SPH, she would feel on the same level as her friends.

Thus for a few months we went to São Paulo Hospital instead of Einstein, until another "It's not fair" incident forced our hand. Meanwhile, our family prepared for a two-month furlough in the United States:

> **Jun 5, 1999** *Time is going too fast, getting ready for two months in the US—I have changed so since last time I was there. I am already sixteen. Sixteen has always before seemed old, almost adult to me. The year of becoming. I am now allowed to date. To drive (at least in the States). In both cases I don't know yet in practice which pedal is the gas and which is the brake.*

Dr. G in São Paulo and Dr. F in Indianapolis agreed Karis should go to Pittsburgh for testing by an intestinal motility specialist. The testing confirmed Karis's intestinal dysfunctions, but to our disappointment, solutions proved as elusive in Pittsburgh as in São Paulo.

In fact, over the summer Karis got sicker. Dehydrated, she nearly passed out on a tour of Wheaton College. We detoured to Indianapolis to consult with Dr. F. Hoping to still make Mansfield, Ohio in time to speak at a mission conference, Dave left Karis and me and our suitcases in the Riley Hospital lobby. We knew no one in Indianapolis.

Dr. F told us Karis needed several weeks inpatient on TPN to regain equilibrium. As she grew stronger, she began visiting other patients: a little girl burned in a house fire . . . a boy with spinal meningitis . . . a toddler recovering from open heart surgery . . .

I, meanwhile, hid in Karis's hospital room and sulked. Or I went outdoors and paced, sobbing and begging God to heal my daughter. I was not a happy camper. In August, one at a time, Rachel and Valerie, fourteen and eleven, flew from Ohio back to São Paulo to begin their school year. Dan started college at Yale. Dave phoned but didn't remember it was my birthday. (Did I mention I was not a happy camper?)

One morning while Karis made the rounds of her patient-friends, a stranger named Sarah appeared in the doorway of Karis's room and invited me to the hospital coffee shop. She told me the following story.

When Sarah's fourteen-year-old daughter Annette understood she was dying, she folded into herself, assumed a fetal position, and refused to talk to anyone. Distressed and desperate, for the first time since childhood Sarah found herself praying. She asked God to send someone who could break through the wall of silence Annette had erected around herself.

The next day, Sarah told me, an angel appeared at Annette's door, dressed in a hospital gown and pushing an IV pole just like Annette's. The angel sat by her bed, stroking her hair and singing to her.

The next day the angel was back, talking gently to Annette, singing to her, praying for her. On the angel's next visit, Annette opened her eyes and saw the angel's smile. In time, Annette began to smile back.

Because God answered her first prayer, Sarah started praying more, as did her mother, Annette's grandma. As we finished our coffee, Sarah invited me to Annette's room. Karis was sitting in bed with Annette, blonde and auburn heads bent together over a Bible from which Annette was reading aloud, their IV poles standing sentry. Annette's grandmother sat nearby with tears running down her cheeks.

Tears flooded my own eyes. I ran outdoors, this time weeping in repentance for my self-centeredness and lack of trust. In response to a desperate mother's plea, God's love reached Sarah and Annette because Karis let his grace shine through her weakness. How could I continue to nurture resentment?

Finally, Dr. F allowed Karis to return to São Paulo on one condition: that she continue TPN there. Karis insisted on TPN at home, rather than in the hospital, a new concept in Brazil. Dr. G advocated for her with a home health care company, and reduced her TPN to twelve hours a day so she could attend classes untethered.

> **Aug 21, 1999** *Home at last! Today I could not get the grin off my face; I was glowing. To be back in Brazil, to see, kiss, hug, walk and talk with my friends again . . . new adventures and much to conquer; restored delight. Your joy is my strength, Lord. As Twila Paris sings, "love's been following me."*

The "new adventures" ahead would require every bit of the joy and strength God would give us. On October 4, Guilherme died, a little boy Karis met at São Paulo Hospital and loved dearly. She wrote a long poem about the experience of losing him. Here are a few lines:

> *My heart will always whisper back its secrets,*
> *and Gui you are one of the sweetest . . .*
> *We have this treasure, you and I,*
> *the treasure of not choosing when to die . . .*

Soon after, Karis spiked a fever and was herself admitted to SPH. Protocol called for removal of her catheter while the line infection was treated. But good quality catheters were scarce in Brazil and Dr. G was already concerned about Karis running out of venous access.[6] After several days of treatment with antibiotics, he decided to use the catheter again for TPN, and placed the order before leaving for his clinic, several miles away.

Within minutes of starting the TPN, Karis began shaking with chills. Her fever soared off the end of the thermometer. Her terrified nurse was too paralyzed to take action on Dr. G's orders over the phone.

Despite my own terror, God empowered me to act. Karis was purple and

---

[6] There are only six veins large enough for a central line to the heart. The irritation of a plastic catheter can cause scarring that eventually makes each vein unusable for central venous access.

shaking so much it took three people to hold her still enough for me to give her an injection. While Dr. G fought rush hour traffic, we packed her burning body in ice and repeated the injection. By the time Dr. G arrived, racing through the hallways, we had done all that could be done. Karis managed to croak, "Good-bye, Mommy" before she was unable to speak at all.

Later, we learned that the youth group at our church had been in a meeting when someone said, "We need to pray for Karis. *Right now.*" They had all gone to their knees and for two hours, begged God for her life. They didn't find out until the next day why they had felt this burden of prayer.

Dave was at home hosting out-of-town guests, pastors of one of our supporting churches. I had trouble finding words to accurately portray by telephone the crisis Karis and I had been through. By the time he arrived at the hospital, Karis was stable, and it seemed to him almost a non-event.

Valerie recalls that evening like this:

> I was eleven, home with Dad and a couple from the US who were visiting us; Rachel had already gone to bed. I was working late on a cardboard model of Corrie ten Boom's home as a visual aid for a book report on *The Hiding Place*. My dad got a phone call from the hospital, and he left suddenly, saying that Karis was very sick and might be dying, and he had to go be with Mom and Karis. So then I was home alone with our visitors, wondering if Karis was still alive and if she would make it through the night. Clearly this was a problem too great for me to deal with, so as I worked I began singing: "I cast all my cares upon you, I lay all of my burdens down at your feet, and anytime I don't know what to do, I will cast all my cares upon you." I sang it over and over again, each time feeling a greater sense of peace and confidence that God was taking care of my sister. This was one of the first times I noticed God clearly taking my burdens and giving me peace amidst circumstances too heavy for me to face. That night, God became my Hiding Place.

I (Debbie) spent the night at the hospital, sitting with Karis after the surgery to remove her catheter until she was stable and able to sleep. The next morning, I met Dave and our American guests at a restaurant for breakfast on their way to the airport. I was tremulous and could hardly eat.

Our guests happily talked about their time in Brazil and their concerns back home. I couldn't focus on what they were saying, and missed a question. "What's wrong with you?" the woman said. "David, does she always get this upset when Karis has problems? Have you two ever considered that maybe Debbie's priorities are out of line, that she's too emotionally involved with Karis, or that she doesn't trust God?"

I got up, walked carefully to the bathroom, and threw up. I didn't say another word to our guests while Dave drove them to the airport, nor to Dave on the way home. I didn't know what words to use to quantify my distress, even to myself. It all seemed too much to deal with. I didn't know I was in shock.

For weeks, I felt the impact of this incident on me. What I had done— taking over emergency care for Karis in place of hospital personnel—was outrageous. The choices I had made, the actions I had taken, circled through my mind over and over and over again. Awake and in my dreams, I couldn't stop analyzing, evaluating, second-guessing. I had to keep looking at Karis to reassure myself she was alive, breathing, no longer burning up with fever, no longer purple and shaking, telling me good-bye. . . .

Later, I researched helpful responses to someone reacting to trauma. I wanted never, ever, to leave anyone else as emotionally abandoned as I felt in the wake of Karis's close brush with death that night.

In the aftermath, Dr. G told Karis she could not stay at SPH; she would have to return to Einstein. "It's not about fanciness, Karis. It's about safety. We do not have the resources here to keep you safe." The ensuing conversation was intense. Behind Karis's resistance to Einstein Hospital was her life-long frustration with the amount of money spent to keep her alive, when in many places there were children starving not because they *couldn't* eat (often Karis's situation) but because they simply didn't have food.

Dr. G drew a line in the sand. "Karis, if you insist on staying at SPH, you will have to find another doctor. This incident was too scary. I will not do it again."

"It's not fair," Karis wept into her pillow. "Can't we somehow take the insurance money and buy food for the children? I bet we could feed the whole continent of Africa! I know what hunger feels like, and I see their faces in my dreams. Please, Mom, how am I to bear this injustice?"

It's true. Life is not fair.

Karis with one of her "Beloveds," her dear Brazilian friend Karina

CHAPTER 6

Promise and Prophecy

Age Sixteen
January 2000
Eleventh Grade at PACA

Rachel knows more about how Karis received the Promise and the Prophecy than I do. Rachel says:

In July 1999, Karis traveled to a small town in Brazil on a mission trip called Promifé (pronounced Proe-me-feh) organized by a group of Baptist churches. She met people there who would be among her "Beloveds" for the rest of her life. Geraldo, Alex, and Yara not only opened up new visions of friendship but new concepts of spiritual fellowship and experience as well.

Karis returned elated and the next time the mission trip occurred (it was biannual during January and July holidays for a week each time), I (Rachel) went too. When Valerie started participating, it became a joint sisters' experience that we cherished.

At Promifé, between 15 and 120 teenagers (it grew over time) slept on the floor of a public school. There was drama around cold showers, especially in the winter month of July. Motherly "tias" ("aunties") from the sponsoring churches prepared delicious Brazilian food three meals a day in the school kitchen. I get hungry just thinking about it.

The week's intensive schedule focused around training, prayer, door-to-door evangelism, Vacation Bible School for town children, and showing the InterVarsity film "Jesus" in public squares in the evening. Bonding was reinforced because of the ways we teens supported each other as we were forced outside our comfort zones. Frequently, a group of US teenagers joined us and Val, Karis and I served as translators, a role I especially loved because it helped me connect despite my social awkwardness.

The most meaningful connections of all happened through times of prayer. Intercession sometimes took hours each day. This was prayer with *soul*, with full Brazilian emotional expressiveness. Fears, anxieties, agony, tears, excitement, joy, hope, worship – prayer times ran the gamut of emotions. Most exciting was when we felt like we heard God speak or saw him act.

A small group of especially enthusiastic prayers would gather to pray after everyone else had gone to bed. Geraldo, Yara and Alex were among them.

In their belief system, spiritual gifts such as prophecy and tongues were active. When they prayed, they expected to hear God speak. It was not uncommon for Alex to pray in tongues and Gera to interpret. One of those times Gera asked me if I understood what Alex was saying. I said no, of course not. Gera started interpreting, and to my surprise it was a message for me! God was telling Alex that he was giving me spiritual gifts. I fell to my knees and silently told God I was not worthy. The next words out of Gera's mouth were "Do not say you are not worthy. I (God) have made you worthy." That was all the confirmation I needed that God was really speaking – how else could Alex and Gera know my inner thoughts and prayers?

Even 17 years later I don't know how to describe the emotions of those experiences. At times it was like… being caught up in a glory of soft liquid gold or an incredible sense of peace or an overwhelming sense of being cared for. It was like being seen – profoundly seen – into the depths of my soul and yet equally treasured. After my first Promifé I went home and told my parents they didn't understand the work of the Holy Spirit because they had never taught us about experiences like that. Years later I came to realize the Holy Spirit didn't have to act quite so dramatically to be present and working – and recognized the multi-faceted evidence of his presence in my parents' lives.

I share this as background for the way Karis received her Promise and Prophecy, also through a prayer time with Alex, Geraldo and Yara. I was not there at the time, but I can imagine from my own experiences how moving and transformative it was. And why she held those personal words from God so close to her heart and had such confidence in their veracity.

And here I give the narrative back to my mom (Debbie):

The Promise: "*Seu Amado está guardado.*" Your Beloved is chosen, reserved, saved, protected, hidden, or set apart for you—the word "guardado" in Portuguese has multiple shades of meaning.

The Prophecy: "*You will be a door many nations will walk through to find Christ. You will be given a key to this door.*"

These words engraved themselves on Karis's heart. From that day on, they shaped her perspective on her life. Karis did not share this with Dave or me (Debbie). I only learned about the promise and the prophecy years later when I read her journals. But they became the lens through which Karis interpreted the events of her life. She believed she would not die until the promise and the prophecy were fulfilled.

The promise grounded Karis and helped protect her romantic imagination through high school and college, when many of her friends followed a different lifestyle. Since her Amado, her Beloved, was chosen and set apart for her, she must also save herself for him. Who this special someone was, where he might be, what language he spoke, what he might be doing this very minute, how God was shaping him . . . the mystery held endless fascination.

Karis believed she would marry her Amado, and they would have a daughter, whom she would name Iris, Silvanna ("silv," wild/untamed + "anna," grace—Karis's name in Hebrew; Nov 24, 2003) or Tikvah (Hebrew, "hope"; Dec 2003).

Once she determined that any given young man was not her "Amado," Karis felt complete freedom to develop a close friendship with him. This sometimes confused and frustrated those young men, which in turn frustrated Karis. *"Why can't he understand the word No? Why can't we just enjoy loving each other as friends? What am I doing wrong?"*

Karis interpreted the prophecy to mean her Amado would have a significant international ministry and she would serve alongside him. Would this be in the Middle East, India, Africa . . .? She was intrigued and curious about what God would do. How could she be a Door? And what was the Key she would receive? How could she best prepare for the exciting life God planned for her?

Though she reflects often on the promise and the prophecy in her journals, Karis kept these words close to her heart, treasuring their import. Even on her toughest days, when the fulfillment of either the Promise or the Prophecy seemed remote and improbable, she knew: she was in cahoots with God!

Our family in 2000: Dave, Valerie, Debbie, Karis, Rachel, Dan

CHAPTER 7

My Daddy Taught Me

Age Seventeen
May 2000-April 2001
Twelfth Grade at PACA

My Daddy taught me ocean and Andes
to throw the fiber of my four feet
onto the sea when it convulses
under torrent and thunder;
strain past the breakers
to the six-meter swells
bellowing at the top of my pea-lungs.
He taught me majesty. He taught me what it is
to be completely out
of control
and beyond fear.
And this has served me better
in my hospital bed
than anywhere
else.
Karis, February 7, 2001

The ocean, the Bolivian Andes . . . these were parts of our family culture that came entirely from David. It was his vision, too, that had brought us to Brazil. June 19, 2000, we celebrated ten years in São Paulo. Our adopted country had given us a new culture and language and friends, a tapestry of unexpected adventures, immense challenges, thrilling delights, and profound sorrows.

Following a month-long family trip to Europe, a surprise gift from friends, Karis mused in her journal about her love for the ocean, part of her birthright from her father, who carried all of his children into the waves when they were infants:

Aug 10, 2000 *The word "ocean" conjures for me so many varied images: the cold waters off the coast of California and warm water of Rio beaches; the tide licking at the New Jersey boardwalk; the surging under the ferry that carried me to the Statue of Liberty; the widening gray expanse between the ferry "Cezanne" and the white cliffs of Dover; the swooping seagulls on every beach everywhere; the pounding of the rising tide just outside my tent at Marataízes; the clear blues and greens* *of the French Riviera; brilliant, breathtaking sunset on the Italian Adriatic; eternal swells meeting the horizon through the round peephole of a plane window; churning foam ripping a body board out from under me, whipping me around like a rag doll, spitting me out on the grating shore, sand in my mouth and hair and eyes . . .*

Always I run and dance with the waves. I believe the rhythm of the beach must have taught the first poets to chant and the dancers to lift their feet. The waves and sand and stars hold for me all that is too numerous to count; deep and beautiful and powerful mysteries that speak rhythm and peace and eternal hope that day comes after night. The tides are like the ocean's breathing; the sea's heartbeat. Beaches mark the passage of the years—they are one of the constants of my life.

As Karis contemplated leaving for college, her home and family became frequent journaling topics.

Aug 12, 2000 *Since I was very little my parents taught me to run to them with my fears and tears, pain and questions and dreams in the night. I don't remember when I began to realize they were only Your shadow and transfer my confidence to You. Oh, Father, all my ways, even the ones no one knows of, I learned from the three of you. Thank you, Father, for this gift of my parents. And for tears.*

Nov 10, 2000 *I'm glad I'm small because Mommy and Daddy's laps will never get too small for me, and I can fit where other people can't, and be held up above a crowd at a show and be thrown, and ride piggyback, and not hit my head when everyone else does. It is not right to ever grow up all the way, so you don't do summersaults when you're happy.*

Dec 1, 2000 *This afternoon I cried for a long, long time and for no reason. I slept, and awoke feeling as if my soul had just stepped out of a bath. Now for a few precious moments the house is empty and silent— except for music and neighbors, dogs and birds and the crunch of gravel outside and the clicking cuckoo clock.*

My house, no matter how empty, is sweet company. Daddy's shoes placed together beside the couch; the kitchen with its warm smells. Each corner and piece of furniture holds memories and hints that people will be right back, and that the people are loved and cared for. Mommy is making secret plans to replace the girls' mirror, which has been cracked for years upon years, for Christmas. And to buy Daddy a couch to replace the broken, frayed, faded green one in the back, with its holes and lumps and the smell of sick cat. Won't it be beautiful! Thank You for the incredible gift of a sane mind, and the other gift of a busy, loving family, and the other gift of this room of my own with a window.

Wednesday, Dec 20, 2000 *So, Lord, is this Your way of answering my plea for rest? I love it! Sitting in the locker hallway waiting for the rain to pass and Daddy to pick me up. Who would turn down a date with You and the summer rain outside? Danny arrives tomorrow morning for Christmas vacation.*

[Later] I sat (actually just flopped, all the muscles in my body made of Becca's finger jello) on the couch. I lay there, flumped, so tired. God, will I ever manage to finish all the college applications? Will I ever spend a week, a month, free? Since morning I felt more like kissing my pillow than the day.

Sometimes I wish I could rip out this long blonde hair and blue eyes and walk the streets feeling safe like Carol. Daddy said he's sure my guardian angel gets a workout. I have seen a fusca [VW bug] following me and today a big guy with a watch on his wrist asked me what time it is. There are so many stories, and now that our car was robbed at gunpoint Daddy wants me to be more cautious than ever. By nature I'm not cautious at all. I smile at strangers and stop to sit on the curb with the street kids and tell them stories. But how can I live suspecting everyone and always fearful?

We had no idea until reading Karis's journals how apt were Dave's words about her guardian angel. Karis outrageously flouted common sense, even sitting on our front steps alone at night or early in the morning, easy prey for kidnappers! Yet she never once suffered personal assault. Amazing, in a world where almost everyone we knew had a story to tell of being the victim of crime. Dan had his watch—for which he had saved his allowance for months—stolen off his arm at gunpoint.

Dec 22, 2000 [Wheaton College] *asked me to write two pages about my faith. I wish I could send them my journals or just open myself up and let them see my heart.*

Here is part of the essay Karis wrote for Wheaton:

My joy does not depend on circumstances. It comes from the ongoing conversation I hold with God, who knows and loves me. I am sick so often that if for a moment I were off my guard, I might crumple inside. It must be like this for everyone, days when sheer outrage, or exhaustion, or boredom, or anxiety stand over you seven feet tall and armed. God has been my shield, His Word my sword—and when I cannot go on, He takes it all, leaving the thrill of His presence, and delight in little things.

Each morning when I wake up I ask God for the joy to make it through the day—and quite literally, His joy is my strength. He knows me completely and has taken away my shame of being known. We do not need words. He knows me. He gives me the strength to get up, the strength to ask for strength.

Christmas Day, 2000 *"Now, precious one, what do you need?" This is the phrase Daddy told us to think, pray, and write about as we lit the white advent candle. We'll discuss this at the beach. It seems a strange question in view of the abundance You have poured out on us. Make us truly grateful. May we never miss a chance to give to those in need.*

Maybe the best gift was the note Danny gave me: "Karis, eu te amo e tenho orgulho de ser o seu irmão" [I love you and am proud to be your brother]. *And Dad's tears as he read my Wheaton essay.*

Christmas. The birthday, the anniversary of the greatest treasure, the greatest miracle this world has ever known. May I understand a bit of the reverence, a bit of the awe and joy and mystery and fearsomeness of that night so many years ago.

Karis devoted her first days at the beach to completing her college applications. On impulse, she decided to include Notre Dame, about which she knew nothing except that a PACA friend was applying there.

Dec 30, 2000 *Last night I grinned calling on Your name, being sure of Your presence. That was such comfort that I forgot what else there was to pray. Like groping in the dark for your Father's hand, and leaning against Him, and suddenly forgetting what it was about the dark that frightened you...*

I've been reading a book about intercession. Is this me, Lord? Is this my ministry, my gift? If so, grow me up to it. Convince me of it. Purify me that I may perform it. Oh, God! My heart beats thrilled fast in me. Could it be?. . . so simple. ☺

Without doubt, intercession was one of Karis's gifts. At least half of the pages in her journals are prayers for her friends and for situations she became concerned about.

Jan 8, 2001 Home *Wow. I had forgotten—forgotten the incredible capacity my body has for pain. Forgotten in my body your comfort and the strength you provide in my weakness. Wow. I didn't know I was capable of surviving that. The night lies before me long yet to endure, but I am glad for the invitation to hear your whispers. I have no energy to write. Father, may I crawl into Your lap and cry a little while, cry joy for the lap? Seventeen, barely begun, trying to learn the world and so weary.*

Jan 13, 2001 *The roses Daddy bought are so beautiful.*

Soon after, in the hospital, Karis returned to one of her favorite themes, dance. Here is a sample:

Last January the rhythm filled me as I stood, my whole body taut with awareness, a few feet from pounding waves beyond which the sun melted into deep thunderstorm hues of the evening sky. I felt the freedom of the huge expanse of wet sand beneath my toes and whispered, "This must be the song that first taught men to dance." So, my heart trilling, my feet licking the waves, I flew lightly with the twilight into night, rejoicing in the wide beach of God's love.

To dance is to join two things so often separate: body and soul. It is for a moment to be fully in one place. To dance is to forget all else and at the same time to bind all that really matters to you and show it to the world. When I have been confined to my bed, still my heart danced, still the breeze was free in the trees and the tide. Even in stillness and silence, if you look into my eyes, you will see the song behind them.

Since at this time she was without a central line, Karis was able to receive TPN only as long as her peripheral veins held out, about two weeks. It was a boost, but not enough to restore solid wellness.

Feb 9, 2001 Home *I feel like a raisin. I need help. Lord! What must I do to banish this haunting mist, this doubt and confusion, this lack of even desire? What must I do to know these days that flow past my fingers like water are worth something?*

Lord, I have so much. The boys said "nasceu num berço de ouro" [born in a golden crib—in English we would say, "born with a silver spoon in her mouth"]. I can breathe. I can pet my cat and dog and feel my fish nipping my finger. They say I'm so strong, such an example. I am only me, nothing to be proud of. Don't they see my empty hands? The joy though is genuine—it's Yours. Papa. Forgive me for my needs. I begin to say this and then realize You made me with these needs.

Feb 11, 2001 SUNDAY *Your day. Mommy came and sat cross-legged with me on my bed. She opened to Psalm 111 and asked me, "Which of these verses does not seem to fit?" I did not hesitate: verse five. In the midst of majestic and glorious deeds: "He provides food for those who fear him."*

Father, You have set me in a time and place unique. If I had been in a different family or country or even city or year, I would not be alive. So many times over You have sustained me and filled me with all manner of good things. I deserve nothing yet I nearly drown in Your grace. My questions dissolve in the honey. Honey in my mouth. You lifting me up. How wise You are! How gentle, how full of mirth.

Feb 14, 2001 *Valentine's Day and I forgot. Could have given Daddy the little wire heart I made . . . He'll be back in a week. Purple carpet of petals on the way home. People so beautiful. Thank you, Lord, for Mr. E not postponing the test or slowing down. That gave me security. Even if it means a bad grade, and losing sleep. The whole world hasn't stopped. When they put up walls I can fling out sobs every once in a while—alone with you—but keep climbing.*

Feb 15, 2001 *My dreams are starting to get mixed up with my waking hours and nothing seems real. There are lapses in my awareness. Writing something then noticing I had already written it, hearing and reading but not comprehending. Feeling safe though, my huge tummy almost hidden, inside Daddy's big green-and-white-striped shirt. The doctor talks about central line again, and the pain that doubles me over and the hunger agree with him. Daddy prayed for me over the telephone.*

I sing, "Everybody has a water buffalo" and "Coconut and bananas" and "skidg-u-murinki-dinky-doo" and "Please don't bring your tyrannosaurus rex to show and tell" and "I've got a button." I watch the beautiful city fly by my window full of light and wind, bridges and beautiful people. I'm glad they're Free. I can open and close my hand and turn in a circle and run my hands through a full head of hair.

I feel older than wrinkles. Younger than bath wrinkles. Absent.

Feb 21, 2001 *The girls came banging in, cheerful, laughing. Rachel and Val—I suppose they haven't changed, but I find myself amazed with them now. At Valerie's skill for memorizing—she's torn between "The Raggedy Man" (my favorite) and "The Bear," both by James Whitcomb Riley. At Rachel's beautiful hair, like Maid Marian's. The strength in their legs,* *the way they keep doing and doing things without tiring, their wit, their carinho [affection], their patience with me.*

Someone clapped at the door [a Brazilian "doorbell"], Roberto and his mother come to pray for me. I searched the musty interior of my mind for a face to put with the name and came up lacking. Smoothed my I-just-got-electrocuted hair, walked into the living room with some trepidation. They left me feeling I had been visited by angels. I wanted to build an altar to remember always this gift. They gave me hope. Energy. A clear mind.

Mar 2, 2001 PACA Senior trip to Brotas[7] *I'm sitting under a wooden framework laden with flowers. Senior trip thus far has been nonstop and unforgettable, from conversations to paisagens [landscapes] to the click of the camera on Tim sleeping in the bus. Soaking rain, sunburn, magnificent stars. Açaí, rappeling and canyoning, white-water rafting and swimming, hiking muddy trails and upstream, standing under waterfalls, climbing trees, praying together. Talita and Tati and I had delicious time together in the hammock until late. We saw a shooting star.*

Mar 5, 2001 *Your strong arms circle me, gently slipping under my armpits and raising me. Songs and tears. Watching the waterfall, the racing horse beneath me, the stars, the dances. Hugs. The worship that fills me is unutterable. Hold to me still and always. Because I am still in the river and the current abates sometimes, but only sometimes. . . . And as Rich Mullins put it, "we are not as strong as we think we are." But You have guarded me with Your life.*

Years later, Karis wrote a poem about this senior trip, called "Brotas." Here are a few lines:

> *Sugarcane is bamboo-strong*
> *and when you streak through a field*
> *and are flung from your horse*
> *it hammocks you down easy . . .*

---

[7] Brotas in the interior of the state of São Paulo, features "adventure tourism."

Afterwards, how can you begrudge these white sterile walls,
these crippled legs?
But how can you endure them?

Only because friends are bamboo-strong,
will reach into the absence of tissue and wipe your nose
with their fingers
and when fear streaks through your sky
and flings you from your grin
they hammock you down easy.

Mar 14, 2001 *Endurance is not just the ability to bear a hard thing, but to turn it into glory. Father, all my body wants is to go back to bed. Could you tell it, it can't? It's not listening to me. It just hurts louder, like one of my CEVAP[8] kids when they hear "no."*

Mar 30, 2001 *So good to sit weak on the couch, peace leaking into what was before fragments. Daddy's strong arms about me. I begin to dare to believe tomorrow will come.*

Apr 7, 2001 *I got acceptance letters from Wheaton and Notre Dame; tried hard to be as happy outside as I was inside. My thoughts are Maypole ribbons soaked by the gale and flapping in the wind. Their color leaks away into pools on the ground somewhere. Help me, Father God!*

I remember Dad's face and voice as he said, "Karis, unless there is a miracle this is not temporary." The thought of "the rest of my life" is a hoop I refuse to jump through. The hope of tomorrow being different is the only thing pulling me through. I can't believe life will always be like this. I can't.

*How can I possibly rise to Your call, **be a door for many to pass through**, hold out my hands prepared and believing to receive my gift; how can I be free to follow You—like this? I can't even meet the most basic expectations.*

---

[8] Karis tutored slum children through CEVAP, a Compassion program at our church.

46

I am discontent. Lord, I wish I could give at least that gift to you, to be content.

Oh, Lord, has self-pity flawed me? Will I ever not be hungry, will I ever be free of pain? When we are weak, then we are strong—is that true?

Shoot. **I have your promises.** *If I believed them I would not be so terrified. Oh, God, I want to believe. I place my hope on Your power to resurrect me.*

Apr 13, 2001 *Daddy was right. Notre Dame is doing too good a job of wooing me. Quality is in everything I see or hear about them. And my desire to leave the cocoon of Christian (Protestant, Evangelical) is acute. Imagine—world renowned authors, researchers, teachers, friends. To find mentors and people who won't be easy on me. Wild—the idea of studying literature, history, dance, in depth. Of learning to judge for myself. Of working. Of walking through the cold with a red nose and having a bike and jogging by the lake. Getting to know all kinds of religions. Oh, Lord, I'm so excited. Just the idea of doing the unexpected and going against some dear people's wishes is exciting.*

Am I strong enough for college? I feel weaker now than a year ago. More skeptical, more wary & restrained. Not outwardly, but there is a lot hidden for lack of proper outlet.

Could I lose my faith? I would rather die. But we are sealed together. They cannot tear us apart without tearing me. Easter is coming! All my own life questions fade to insignificance and I am in awe of You, of Your safe wide beach.

Watching Karis make plans for college while on many mornings she couldn't even get out of bed felt surreal. It required of me a conscious "suspension of disbelief" and a daily decision to trust God. Easy? No. Not at all. Might another surgery be part of God's provision for her? Dr. F thought it possible.

Karis was rattled at first by the standing ovation she received at her high school graduation. Suddenly, though (after this photo was snapped), her face cleared. She pointed up and started clapping too. She told us later that she figured out everyone was clapping for God.

CHAPTER 8

Lord, I Need a Backbone

Ages Seventeen and Eighteen
April-August 2001
Indianapolis and São Paulo

Dr. G, our beloved doctor in São Paulo, disagreed with Dr. F in Indianapolis about whether surgery might help Karis. Dr. F's optimism gave Karis hope for real change. But it felt like a betrayal of Dr. G.

Before the surgery in Indianapolis, we visited the University of Notre Dame, our first time there. In stark contrast to Wheaton and the Ivy League colleges we had visited, ND's attitude was, "If you choose to come here, we will do everything possible to make it work for you." Even thinking about college at that point was an act of faith that somehow, by August, Karis would be well—or at least well enough. At ND, I felt God saying to me, a mother deeply worried about her child, "Trust me. I love your little girl, even more than you do." Could I do so? *Would* I trust him, even in this?

Waving good-bye to Dave, Rachel, and Val at the São Paulo airport on April 19, Karis and I expected to be gone just a couple of weeks. God had taught me about his sovereignty the last time we were at Riley (see the story in Chapter 5). This time I was determined to practice Psalm 145:2, "Every day I will bless Thee," actively looking for what God was doing around me each day we spent in Indianapolis.

> **Apr 21, 2001 *Lord, I need a backbone***. *Or that's what I think I need. This last semester has been a chiseling away of me, thoroughly humbling.*

April 27, as she was wheeled to the OR at Riley Hospital, Karis asked me to mail her acceptance card to Notre Dame, an act of courage and of hope. The surgeon found Karis's abdomen so full of scar tissue she changed her mind about removing a section of intestine. It took hours to tease out those pesky adhesions, but Dr. W believed Karis's intestinal function would improve dramatically. Mid-surgery, Dave walked into the waiting room! A Brazilian friend had persuaded him he should be with us.

Five days post-surgery:

> **May 2, 2001** *Nothing very profound to say. But there are so many bright spots of joy I can say I am all right. My energy is returning. They've*

pulled down most of the scaffolding needed to build wellness back in, so now all that's left is my central line. Free arms, legs, face, back!

Dad was there when I came out of anesthesia! Mom and Dad got a kick out of me. I was pumped full of drugs, incisions and tubes, my voice a hoarse scratch, but bubbly and chatty. Dad commented this might be what I'd be like if I ever get drunk.

The day after her eighteenth birthday and nine days post-surgery, with her father back in Brazil, Karis reflected:

May 6, 2001 *I'm still here in the hospital. It's a strange thought—Sunday. Rachel and Valerie are probably chatting with a group of guys on the way back from church or trying to choose a chicken from the Rotisserie up at the padaria* [bakery]. *Dad will arrive excited about all that went on at church, and if Rachel made the rice it will be burnt or too salty and they'll all laugh and survive.*

Yesterday was the most incredible day. Jane [a friend from Brazil now living in Indy] *pulled off a surprise birthday party for me, and I got to see their three kids. I was overwhelmed with generosity, like a spectator of one of God's special secrets, His love pouring over me. All day was this flood of people, and 26 emails, and cards & balloons & flowers till we ran out of places to put them.*

May 11, 2001 *Friday. Two weeks since surgery. How much longer it seems! My birthday balloons and flowers have begun to droop. Down in the courtyard where Mama and I looked long at the fountain and eternal flame I cried for missing home, for fearing the future, for the CF* [Cystic Fibrosis] *patient down the hall who was only seventeen when she died. For all the pain and pressure I haven't let out. It was good. Beautiful in the moonlit breezy garden.*

My body is weak, very hungry. But I can't handle food. Amy is gone. We were together for days, Amy and I. We played games: "Amy, let's see if you can be quiet for one minute . . . for two minutes . . ." She called me "Karis Kornfield who lives in a cornfield."

May 16, 2001 *Last night I threw up all the progress we had made.*

This was Karis's last journal entry for eleven days. Here is what happened:

After performing Karis's first surgery, Dr. W took a leave of absence because her mother died. The doctor who assumed Karis's care in her place expected Karis to recuperate faster than she did. He decided her failure to eat was psychosomatic: Karis didn't actually <u>want</u> to get well (!). When Karis tried to eat, however, she vomited horrible bilious (green, bile-stained) stuff from her intestine. I couldn't imagine how Karis could "fake" the abdominal distention and pain she was experiencing.

This doctor had no sense of humor. One day, to break the ice with him, Karis painted each of her toenails a different color. When she heard him coming, she put her head under the covers and her feet on her pillow. The doctor just stood there tapping his foot, saying, "Come on, Karis, I don't have all day."

I insisted on further testing. Instead, the doctor referred Karis for a psychiatric consult. Anxious and angry, I appealed to Dr. F. He ordered immediate barium x-rays, which showed severe bowel obstruction. Dr. W came back from her leave (thank you, Lord!) to perform emergency surgery that saved Karis's life.

Recuperation from this second major surgery was grueling, physically and emotionally. The trauma of the bowel obstruction and emergency surgery impacted Karis profoundly, and she referenced it in her journal for years afterward.

> **May 27, 2001** [Eleven days post-op] *Dear Lord, help me. I don't remember how to pray. I don't know what happened, what is happening—but it has to stop.*

> **May 29, 2001** *Going home soon. Afraid to write that. Crossed fingers an expression of hope hope hope hope please please please please please. The emails I receive from PACA friends scare me. If scare is the right*

word. What is going on, Lord? They're making it sound like I'm some sort of hero.

Maybe some of my tears have to do with my fear of myself. People say I'm strong, I'm a hero. And that's what I don't know what to do with. I am nowhere near those things. I've been remembering the bowel obstruction, how they lay me down and the black seeped through the edges of my vision, my whole frame aching, the vomiting, the blind lightheaded agony. I thought I could not hold up under it. But You in Your infinite gentle understanding brought me through.

Lord, should I accept PACA's offer of exemption from the rest of my fourth quarter work? It's like running a race with a terrible cramp and not giving up, and then <u>this</u> <u>close</u> to the finish line being told "it's OK, you don't have to finish." Oh Father, don't you see I'm not insane to want to do the work? Yet such an incredible gift . . . Mommy cried when she read the e-mail. Freedom for time with friends and the millions of little things I'd love to do; freedom for the time central-line care will require . . .

Our June 4-5 journey back to São Paulo was my most challenging travel experience to date. Karis became very ill, with rash and fever. **"Every** day I will bless Thee . . ."? But arriving home in time for her graduation from PACA meant so much to Karis that the stressful journey "didn't matter." Karis had three days to recover from the trip before that milestone day, twenty-four days after her second surgery.

Jun 6, 2001 Home!! *After six weeks away it's like rediscovering life to be home & gaining energy & movement. I must admit I'm sick of being honored and receiving presents. These things are meant to be done in small doses. When you're sick and gone, and have your birthday and graduate all in one month . . . Well, you mean & say an awful lot of thank yous, every other one to your Lord.*

During the ceremony or at the party afterward, Karis's surgical incision split open. She didn't tell anyone, not wanting to miss a moment of her celebration. The incision got infected, and for several weeks—her break between high school and college—Karis was confined to bed rest, with painful wet-to-dry dressing changes three times daily to gradually heal her belly from the inside out. The blessing of PACA's generosity in forgiving Karis's missed weeks of school became fully evident as she was forced to rest.

During this recuperation time, Notre Dame informed Karis that despite having been too sick to complete the required qualifying essay, she had been selected for the honors program! Thirty freshmen were chosen from the College of Humanities and another thirty from the College of Sciences. Karis would have the security of belonging to a small, close-knit community of exceptional students, a refuge as well as launching place for her on a campus of thousands in the strange new world of the United States of America.

Meanwhile, Karis continued to struggle with the trauma of her experience in Indianapolis. It shook her to her core.

> **Jun 14, 2001** *Lord, where did the girl go, the one who believed? And who has taken her place? Oh, Father God, see this, hear me, answer me, I can't stand this other me. The thought of another Wednesday night* [May 16, when she was rushed to emergency surgery] *chills me through. Terrifies me. It was horrid. Oh Lord, what do I need that I might believe in You again? I go through the motions because I used to believe. There once was a me who hoped in You. Who knew You. Who trusted You.*
>
> *I need You now, in my new reality. I need to know You more intimately. I need to return to the days of constant conversations. I need to lose the cynicism that has invaded me. I <u>need</u> . . . I <u>am</u> <u>needy</u>. I'm asking You, Lord, what is real. Until I know, I feel unfit to go on. Do You understand? I can't.*
>
> *I'm screaming, do You hear me? It is to call Your attention. Speak to me, I beg You, Master of the Universe. I want to reach out to You for comfort but I realize now I reach toward a lion. The Dangerous One. The One who allowed so much distress—too much for this vulnerable lamb.*

Jul 2001 *The real me does not just lie in this bed. Hope scratches and hollers as it's packed away for Maybe Never.*

Jul 11, 2001 *Pardon my handwriting. I'm back in the hospital on account of a fever and the IV is in my right knuckle. Dems da breaks.* ***I have an ardent desire for a rod strong within me*** *to inspire action, take initiative, hold the things I know and am so I might serve You rather than react like a child, so upset. Sei que passará logo tudo isso* [I know all of this will soon pass] *but for right now something chokes me. Sticks in my throat and makes me restless.*

Jul 18, 2001 *I feel imprisoned, in an ivy tower. I have been living basically at home or in the hospital since this year began. I want to walk, to walk and walk until I fall. I sobbed so completely unlike a baby last night, for a multitude of no reasons.*

Jul 19, 2001 *One month. Exactly one month from now I am to take off for the U.S. Last night Danny came in and asked why his sister was so melancholy. My spirits must relearn the dance.*

Jul 23, 2001 *A gentle song should accompany this moment rather than the scratchings of an old pen. A new era—I know in most practical ways it begins on August 19th, but in some ways, it begins here. Dr. A pulled my catheter this morning! For the first time in—how long?—I climbed into bed without sterilizing or injecting or priming . . .*

The significance of this "new era," Dr. A pulling Karis's central catheter, cannot be overstated. It meant Karis was finally well enough to nourish herself orally. She could leave for college without all the work and worry of caring for a central line. She could feel and look much more "normal" when she arrived on Notre Dame's campus for her huge transition to the United States and to independent college life.

Aug 16, 2001 *I was thinking about You, Lord, and the natural laws You set—and how solemn a thing it is for You to break them—and when You do, we call that a miracle.*

Writing that, I quite unexpectedly stumbled upon myself fighting for breath, overcome again with such pain, such pain . . . And all that saved me was God, and prayers of Christ's body and the purpose strong enough that God would choose to break His rules. [It seems she was experiencing a flashback.]

*That is why death holds no sting for me. It is not the groundless "invincibility" they say belongs to the young in particular. You stooped to speak with me. To let me know there are angels guarding me, **the keys to myself, a door to many, through which they will come to salvation**. I wonder if I could possibly escape this destiny, even if I were to wander. Jonah in the end could not.*

During these days of contemplating her move to the United States, changing countries, changing cultures, Karis wrote an essay about culture. Perhaps it helped her find the understanding and courage she needed for the uprooting and re-rooting that lay before her. Here is a small excerpt:

What language do you sneeze in? What language do you dream in? What language does the wind whisper in your ear? If you cannot understand the importance of these questions, perhaps you will not understand my fear of returning to the land where I was born… How will I go from a people who dance and kiss and hug, who consider tears a gift, who are forever late and forever passionate and forever young—to the "home" where friendships have grown shallow and people seem always too busy? Going back for college, I want to recapture an understanding of America.

A potpourri of images floats before me: a monkey playing with my hair in a canoe on the Amazon, skyscrapers stretching past the horizon in the city of twenty million I call home, bonfires and caipira dances during the Saints' feasts, fireworks and feasting at midnight on Christmas Eve… Countless traditions, countless ways of preserving the beauty and creativity God has deposited in his multicolored collage of beloved people.

For Karis, this was always what mattered most: the "beloved people" she found wherever she lived, wherever she traveled. It would be no different in the new world of Notre Dame University.

Karis with her beloved Notre Dame roommate, Pranati

CHAPTER 9

Mom, I Think I'm in Heaven

Age Eighteen
August 2001-May 2002
University of Notre Dame

A few weeks into her first semester at Notre Dame, thrilled with the resources available for her current research interest, Karis called me from the Hesburgh Library to exclaim, **"Mom, I think I'm in heaven!"** It was a turning point, a tipping of the balance toward loving and accepting rather than struggling against the complex, terrifying, marvelous, intriguing reality that was Notre Dame.

ND offered Karis myriad opportunities for bridging cultures, nationalities, religions: Brazil to the United States and to dozens of other nationalities. Protestant to Catholic and to Hinduism, Islam, Buddhism, Atheism . . . Event-orientation to time-orientation, and a different sense of personal space, of understanding relationships and expressing affection, different priorities and values, gestures and expressions, foods, ways of dressing, rhythms of life, and so much else that distinguishes world views and cultures.

Karis rejoiced and thrived in the rich mosaic of human experience at Notre Dame. She welcomed the challenge of adaptation, eager to decipher this strange new world quickly so she could then help students from around the world who knew less than she about how to function in the United States.

After orientation weekend, I left Karis glowing, running off to an activity with new friends. "Bye Mom! Have a good trip home!" Karis wrote in her journal those first days:

> *Memories of this first week: the ecstasy of biking in the rain, running into Anthony on my bike and scraping knees & knuckles, so many names flying at me splat on my windshield so I can't see.*

Friends loaned Karis a wonderful bike to use on campus. Karis didn't know how to ride it, for the hills, traffic, and crime of São Paulo had not been conducive to cycling. On her first attempt, gaining a shaky sense of balance, she saw people ahead of her and realized she didn't know where the brake was. She yelled, "Watch out, I don't know how to stop!!" and people got out of the way—all but Anthony, who didn't believe her. He thought it was a prank—until she knocked him down.

Anthony was an American who had grown up in Turkey. Abuelita (Dave's mother) had heard through the expat grapevine that he also would be an incoming freshman honors student. Before Karis even met him, Abuelita already believed Anthony would be a special person in Karis's life. When I commented on Karis's first week at ND, Abuelita's only question was, "Has she met Anthony yet?"

Pranati, Karis's roommate from India, used prostheses for legs. Both girls were thrilled to have a roommate with physical challenges. Pranati lost both legs in the same childhood car accident that stole her mother, father, and sister. She was raised by her aunt and uncle.

> *Pranati is asleep in front of me. Beautiful, strong, so gentle and confident. I am privileged to have her as my roommate. She is Hindu; long black braid and piercing eyes and slender, elegant fingers.*

Karis's e-mails home were full of excitement about the people she was meeting, her classes and professors, her fascination with dorm life and extracurricular activities. She confided feelings of culture shock and homesickness to her journals, not to us. And though she was able to eat and free from TPN, she still struggled to manage this aspect of her life.

Notre Dame offered such wealth: interaction with professors on the cutting edge of their fields of scholarship; visiting lecturers of the highest caliber from around the globe. . . . Once Karis hit her stride academically, she flourished like a garden in springtime.

> **Sep 4, 2001** *I don't shine in this place. I feel like a mortal among gods. Walk beside me this day, guide me, give me strength and joy that stem from Yourself. And make me a blessing to someone.*

9/11 rocked the campus; Karis had a different reaction.

> **Sep 11, 2001** *Somehow the World Trade Center, the Pentagon, Pennsylvania—somehow it did not shock me. Vivid imagination allowed me to fear and to mourn. But it wasn't shocking. Maybe I had no peaceful little world to shatter in the first place. All grief in me still*

falls back on the name Rebeca [a little friend from São Paulo Hospital whose death hurt Karis deeply]. *Sometimes I feel the presence of Your angels protecting & comforting, so close. The joy I asked for is here.*

Oct 01 *Last night as I lay down to sleep I slowly grew into consciousness of what was making me unhappy. I've been trying to fit myself into this world, to make myself lovable and interesting—rather than the other way around, seeking to love. Back we come always to St. Francis's prayers. Lord, may I seek rather to love than to be loved . . .*

The effectiveness of this change of focus quickly became evident. Many of Karis's classmates told me later they had never felt loved as Karis loved them.

Oct 18, 2001 *There is something I can learn here at Notre Dame that will make me better, more useful for the rest of my life. I will not be another young thing bumping around, showing off, joking, panicking when work is due, being cheerful and friendly to all and good to my friends, only these things. I will become more. I will chase after Wisdom. Oh Lord, aside from the desire to know You and to bring You glory in my life, here is my desire:* **to be a helpmate to a great man**, *together to minister to Your Beloveds, together to build a home in each other's hearts like my parents have. If only I could be as happy as they . . . Oh! I want to learn to drive.*

The change of seasons at Notre Dame was an endless source of delight to Karis, who had not experienced this since moving to Brazil at age seven.

Oct 23, 2001 *I watched the ducks leave the lake, and wandered around campus admiring all the trees posing in the nude. Caught a delicious whiff of pine-smell. It should snow this Friday!*

Nov 2001 *Skirt swishing flip around nylon ankles, arms squeezed around myself in locked almost painful attempt to keep out the cold. The darkness fries the grimace onto my face, but tears are too dangerous— why risk crying and being seen by Whoever?*

*Do you know why I'm really crying? Because **I'm afraid I'll never write anything worth publishing, nothing that will reach out and Touch**—and that fear hurts worse than death.*

Nov 18, 2001 *Pop-pop's firm voice teaches me a lesson I was too respectful not to put in my mouth and too stubborn to swallow for a long time later—do not approve of a disdainful mocking attitude, no matter what side of the question you find it on. Do not laugh only because something is funny. Do not unaware set off down the road to narrow-mindedness.*

Her brother Danny (now "Dan") visited Karis at Notre Dame for a few days toward the end of her first semester, which coincided with his Junior year at Yale. Here is a partial account of that visit in his words:

It was so fun to encounter Karis for the first time as a college student, both of us together now in this dramatically new chapter of life. I sat in on some of her honors classes, which had great professors and great reading lists, and suddenly I could share so much with her – about literature, philosophy, friendships, broken hearts, discoveries, doubts, explorations. All of this was perhaps to be expected, but what surprised me was her presence on campus between classes. She knew so many people as we walked across campus, and interacted with them with such loving familiarity.

She was incredibly active. In just a few days and evenings we dashed from a monopoly game in a sunlit nook in her dorm, to a drive with friends in the dark to snow-covered dunes, to a coffee shop where she met a friend teaching her to speak French (she would soon also undertake Arabic), to a "Brazil night" she helped organize with samba dancing, to working in a dining hall, to someone's Mustang which roared us to an off-campus party where neither of us felt very comfortable, to a Catholic mass, to introducing me to Pranati, to a snack time with other honors students, to a run around Saint Mary's Lake, to a quiet evening where she needed to do homework (also she felt very sick that night). She was engaging in immersive activities but her treasure was the people around her – and they could feel it. It was not surprising to me to later discover that her journals were full of prayers for many names, and that she often knew their intimate sorrows and joys. I was amazed at my little sister.

Unfortunately I made some comparative remarks about Yale vs. Notre Dame which I thought were interesting. Through her journal I later discovered that my comments dampened her enthusiasm for my visit. For me it was natural to compare aspects of one college experience with another. I don't think I meant for it to sound critical, but I was not as careful about this as I wish I had been, a sorrow I carry with me. She was left with the impression that I thought I was coming from something better. My true impression was that Notre Dame was a phenomenal environment. And more important, that Karis was blossoming there into a person who left me feeling very lucky and proud to be her brother. I could always be close to her, even after the college years were left behind.

Many of Karis's friendships would also endure. Years later she continued to receive phone calls in her hospital room in another city, often not calling to cheer her up so much as to ask for her wisdom and advice.

One day Karis saw an elderly man sitting on a bench. With a few minutes to spare and thinking he looked lonely, she sat down and struck up a conversation. To her surprise, he was Father Hesburgh, President Emeritus of Notre Dame! Their friendship thrived throughout Karis's years at ND.

Dec 10, 2001 *I had dinner with Father Hesburgh today.*

Dec 2001 *It snowed today. The whole morning was delicious. Walked through the rain to South Dining Hall, met Kyle on the way, set off for the bookstore, when the rain turned soft—white—I couldn't stop trembling, like Buddy, for the joy. Kyle and Sean, Kate and Beth taught me to tango leaving footprints in the slush all over campus like children, hat on the snowman, snowball brushing past Ky's forehead. I forgot completely about my shift at South Dining Hall.*

December 2001 *The world for a little while crumbled. I felt tears dripping off my face before I thought to pay attention to what my eyes were doing and stop them. Here people hide any hurt behind beer or doors. I know no one even still to whom I can go with my foolish frustrated homesickness.*

[Later] Papa, this semester went kind of splat! all over—but I've had loads of fun, started some potentially lifelong friendships, learned way more than I ever imagined there was to know about philosophy and chemistry. I have kept myself pure in terms of clean lips (swearing), physical affection, drinking, dressing modestly, etc.

I have honestly questioned things I heretofore took for granted; learned to be comfortable dancing in public, to swing and tango, waltz and rap. I have read countless interesting books, learned new words, learned better to use the Internet; done well at work. I have learned about India and Spanish, about Africa; gotten to know and cherish my extended family far more; gotten better at guitar—

I will not go on. A list of accomplishments is useless. I will always find people to top such a list. My living is not for these; they are simply things I've noticed have happened along the way.

Home for Christmas, Karis regaled us with stories of people and events and all she was learning. We were thrilled to see her thriving! Dr. G told us that apparently the surgery her senior year had been the right choice. It was healing for us to feel we were back on the same page with him.

Jan 12, 2002 *Today. Today I go. After the time at the beach, after intense heart-cries, unveiled face, on the couch with Daddy holding me . . . after time with so many loved ones, I am more ready to leave than I was a week ago, by a long shot. But still, it tears. I'm pretty sure I'll cry.*

Three weeks at home, and then the return to her other world: whiplash. Some people handle this by not giving themselves to the second world. Karis by nature couldn't do that. Wherever she was, she was all there, adapting to and loving her new environment; breaking down barriers and building bridges.

As Notre Dame embraced her, and as she discovered the Beloveds God had for her there, she loved back with typical Karis-passion. Her second semester at ND was rich in friendships, intellectual exploration, and insights. She journaled prolifically. When as a freshman she won second place in a campus-wide essay competition, the professor who presented her award predicted she would publish her first novel by the time she graduated from ND. A pottery class gave her rich imagery for her poetry. Karis shared all of this with Rachel when she visited on her own college search tour.

At the same time, however, Karis's intestine was gradually giving her more trouble again. She did not tell Dave and me, far away in Brazil. Her symptoms became acute during the summer term, when she took intensive physics and dated a young man I am calling Philip. Earlier in the spring, she had to face the possibility that she could not become a doctor, her dream since childhood.

Mar 2002 *Papa, I heard a word, and I guess I don't yet <u>need</u>, but I would like to know—*

The word "impossible." Dean N said more in a matter of minutes than most people have to me in months. Practical and all out there. Her cordial concern for my health. She looked at me when I said "I know med school will be hard" and retorted, sizing me up, "Maybe impossible. Very likely impossible." And told me why! I wanted to kiss her, too, for giving me such an honest gift of awareness. I know I can take my honest concerns to her because she won't fudge or mince for me.

Impossible. Of course she's right, it is very likely impossible, though no one has had the grace to tell me as much. There is no one who knows, of course, whether it will be impossible. Except for... You. So, Lord, I know that to say "I need to know" is silly, immature. I "need" very little. But in Your time, let me know... Is med school impossible for me?

Apr 27, 2002 *Dear Professor,*

I just received your e-mail, and I understand what you said about taking 50% off of each of my lab reports turned in after the last day. You seem not to have understood my e-mail though. You said I should have let you know beforehand that I was going to miss the lab, and given my report to another student to turn in.

How, Professor? How could I possibly? Do you not understand what it means to fight to stay alive, to be working on a chem lab for hours and get nowhere because the pain short-circuits your mind and doesn't let you comprehend concepts that at other times would have made simple sense?

I hate writing this. I try so, so hard to be okay, to keep going, to avoid asking for sympathy or favors from professors. Do you know—I didn't, not at first—how it tears to know that I've quit? To tell person after person, no, I'm not doing premed anymore, I quit. I was sick.

Yes. No. I am and am not better. It is day in day out forever. I do not pity myself. I beat myself instead. I am a fool. But still I live. I breathe and learn and love and dance. I stay up past midnight, barely have time to sleep, to shower. I am not doing well. Am. Am not.

Apr 29, 2002 *I will do badly. In calc. In chem. Two of the four that remain, finished badly. Perhaps three. No laughter to go with the words, "Ah, I tried my hardest," or even to accompany, "It doesn't matter." No "oh, well" will drip no matter how hard I squeeze this soul of mine.*

Karis received B's in both calculus and chemistry—this was "doing badly" for her and not good enough for pre-med. In her other classes, she earned A's.

And as I fail there are no mother's arms, wrapping me in a warm blanket away from it all. I watch tomorrow approach, arms out, open-palm to receive its due, and I am exhausted, beaten to a pulp. Oh God, may I run to the end. And fall on Your grace. Even with the knowledge that I have lost. Restore me for Your name's sake.

May 5, 2002 *My birthday. 19. Negligible fact. So much good work to do, too much for one day. Oh, thank you, Lord, for strength. Lord—do you remember how once **You told me I would be a door**? How can I learn to discipline myself and become the person You would have me be? Ready, truthful, when? When will You give me the wisdom I need to hold Your Name high? You called me Your beautiful child and poured out Your grace. Perfect, mighty God of the Universe, unleash Your strategy in me.*

May 2002 *Anthony prayed for me. I asked for understanding of what God was doing in my body.*

What *was* God doing through the illness again assailing her? Karis remembered her PACA friend Tati saying, "Don't ask why. Ask what for."

Karis wasn't actually there when this family photo was taken
on the New Jersey shore—she was photoshopped in later!
Back: Dave, Deb, Dan; Front: Valerie, Rachel, Karis

CHAPTER 10

A Task Too Large for Me

Age Nineteen
May–August 2002
Notre Dame Summer Term

At her friend Vera's home on Dauphin Island during the break before summer term, Karis wrote:

May 14, 2002 *The thoughts of whether or not to go into medicine were like a fish, for the nth time reeled in and thrown back to the waves, once again, struggling feeble, dragged across the sand to me, with too many punctures, bleeding from the mouth and yet alive. The thought occurs to me that we haven't tried frying it yet. But then once fried if the fish is no good for eating we have killed it.*

During the summer of 2002, Dave, Rachel, Valerie, and I spent a few weeks traveling in the United States to visit friends and family. The girls and I stopped by Notre Dame for a quick visit to Karis June 23-25 while Dave visited his parents in Florida. Her phone and e-mail communication had been all positive, so I was surprised to find her not doing well.

Jun 25, 2002 *Mama has voiced some concerns. Why must I be sick, of all days, on Mama's coming? I was to be strong and well, a comfort to her mother-heart. I was too weary to answer.*

As Karis studied intensive physics, and dated Philip, her health struggles too became intense.

Jul 4, 2002 *Moonlight, sliver-light, blue-light from the bay windows, collapsed on the stairs. Dark waters flowing out of me in rigid spurts.*

> *My life was to be a river, flowing all*
> *transparent to the same see,*
> *with depths,*
> *but one unashamed body. To love with.*
> *But do you see her wailing, in the corner? . . .*
> *They worry. They should.*
> *My body is no respecter of suns*
> *or independence days.*

I am not wise when I am this weary.

Jul 5, 2002 *Physics exam done, and done well, I hope. The end of a marathon.*

Jul 6, 2002 *Oh, God! Oh—thank you, thank you, thank you. . . No words. Such a gift, a whole night of sleep. It's been weeks. How good You are to me!*

Everything for a moment crashed down into sense! Eleven pounds I lost—they weighed me at the clinic. No wonder I was so hungry! No wonder I ate even though it seemed to destroy me! I needed that nutrition, need . . . No wonder my clothes are loose, my bones and muscles peeking.

Jul 2002 *The doctor wants me to pay attention to the pain. Papa, I won't live if I don't ignore the pain. It makes me want to die.*

I'm not well. Not just physically but in my else-self, whole self, I suffer inexpressible pain. I cannot sort out guilt trips from responsibility, nor reconcile the difference between the way things are and the way I want to live. When I am with people I mostly forget myself. At night, or alone, it engulfs me.

God, give me all I need for life and godliness. I am desperate—

Clearly, things were getting out of control for Karis, but some stubbornness inside made her refuse to "give in" and tell us. I think for her that would have meant admitting that at some level her illness had beaten her. What follows is not easy reading. Karis was in a deep hole emotionally as well as physically. Dave and I, unaware, were traveling around the country reporting on our mission work and visiting friends and family.

When Rachel read this in Karis's journal, she wrote to me, "Why was Karis so convinced she couldn't tell us???? I don't expect anyone to answer that." Why indeed, Karis? Did you fear we would pull you out of college, away from your beloved Notre Dame?

Jul 9, 2002 Physics 2 *"How are you?" Amiable Professor J. My mouth was full of acrid vomit. I could not answer. If I were to smile it would press itself out between the cracks in my teeth. Choice. Intense effort. I swallowed, smiled.*

"Fine. How are you?"

He looked at me, and I wondered if he imagined the grimace behind the mask. This time it really was a mask. The acid burned down my throat, filled my nostrils. I turned, shoved my fist in my mouth and bit, hard, to hold in the pain. I flew into the bathroom, dropping my backpack, into the stall. Thud. Thud. Thud. My head slow against the wall, my fingers wrapped white-knuckled around the metal.

Jul 10, 2002 *I flee him in desperation, El Animal, El Hambre [the Hunger]. With each bite I scream, I gasp my desire to live. With each reverent, fearful, angry, defiant bite—the disappearing food, the clearing plate, I run from the fangs of hunger. Yet I know what I am doing to myself.*

Papa, without Philip yesterday the pain would have been absolutely unbearable. His concern was real, deep. If I had had the energy, I would have reassured him and kept him from it. As it was I trusted him, rested my head in his lap, and slept, my hand white-knuckled around his fingers.

So baby, another today to the tune of pain. Be hero now, in this little way, in this way bigger than you. Call on your God. He is strong. And then be silent hero, hero only to your God, in the place where your throat screams thirst and nobody knows. Inhabit this world in the weakness of His strength. Now slow, take one thing at a time in this secret place while you are still alone and conquer; this day lies before you. Do not rest now. Vomit if you need to, in between; but make your arms strong for their tasks. He hears. Go to Him.

[Later] *Lord, I try. Perhaps not hard enough. But my mind is not so willing as my body to comply. God, I know not how to pray. I sink into* *survival. I forget to enjoy, to understand, to really see the people around me. Beneath my silence is a constant entrapped wailing. Why or where it comes from I do not know. I need to know.*

I do not have the time to write this.

Jul 2002 *I know I have to keep living. But oftentimes, like this afternoon, I forget why and only long to go . . . It's only these that hold me here: faith in the idea God had in putting me into this moment, time & place; love for those who would not understand were I to give up and who would grieve; stubbornness over the clearly unfinished work;* **the now and tomorrow working out of His plan for me.** *My stubbornness is a clinging to faith and hope. These are vision. Blurry, just about to go under, but enough. They remain. As do I. God have mercy. Hallelujah.*

Jul 2002 *Lord, I have to keep my balance as I walk this crest-of-roof with my fiddle* [as in "Fiddler on the Roof"]. *But look who I've employed! On the one side Complainer, on the other, Mocker. So what if on the surface I never complain? Here I am at the mercy of these two. The one knows the depth of my pain and need, the other laughs at it and reminds me how much more others hurt and need. One is self-centered pathos, the other high-pitched mimicking whine. Lord, how can I rid myself of them?*

God, in sleep renew me and make me believe again the bravado that like a mouthful of marshmallow, empty, claims to be glad to be alive.

There won't be strength, you see, not today or tomorrow, and I will fail what I have begun. And in the end I will not be a doctor. I am emptied, thus, with no pride left. Despair saps the little strength that should be in my bones . . .

Mama, Mama, it's not my body, it's my spirit—see? Someone crushed it. I didn't see who or when, the car. But see, I found it here, like roadkill. I've been trying for days to scrape it off the road, to gather the pieces and stuff the parts that exploded back under the skin, soft fur . . . but the stench is beginning to suffocate, and I—

Turn silently to hold myself out, the beautiful self so many have rejoiced in. I can only babble that I don't know what happened, don't know what to do . . .

I sensed rather than knew that Karis was not well. Leaving Dave and the other girls, on July 23, I traveled to Indiana. Mid-afternoon on a bright summer day, I walked into the house where Karis was staying and found her in a fetal position in bed with all the shades drawn. I climbed into bed with her and held her while she sobbed, long, shuddering, wordless sobs from the depth of her soul.

Even then she did not tell me the intensity of her struggle nor her profound desire to quit, to go Home to heaven. I only learned these things through reading these journal entries, scratched out in child-printing, not her beautiful cursive. But gradually the tone of her journaling lightened.

Jul 24, 2002 *My mother is here. What else matters? I start a new chapter, like one reborn. I know that little or nothing actually changed; my body is the same, but somehow believing itself capable again of caring for itself, of finding things that perhaps can be controlled; trying again to live this life.*

Jul 29, 2002 *The time has finally come to fry the fish. To step out in faith into the else He has for me. In some ways it is terrifying; yes, Philip was right when he asked me if this, "being a doctor," hadn't been the dream I built my life around. Yes, for as long as I can remember, almost.*

It hurts to let go, but it's immensely freeing, too. Oh, how humbling, to relinquish my own dream for His better one! And how I wanted mine! But I, child of grace, created to do good works He prepared in advance [Ephesians 2:10]—I was not fashioned for this. Philip bled for me, understood my embarrassment and my fear and my resolution, gathered me in his arms. Lord, Your work proceeds.

On July 28, our family traveled to Ventnor, NJ for a Kornfield family reunion. We had three big events to celebrate: Abuelita's eightieth birthday, Dan's twenty-first birthday, and Dave's parents' fiftieth wedding anniversary. Karis stayed at ND to complete her second physics intensive, joining us after her final exam, August first.

Jul 30, 2002 *Papa. I greet the good blurry morning. I seem to have lost my ability to keep my exhaustion inside. It is round and blue and under my eyes. I can't fake it anymore. Did You call me this summer to be a failure?*

Philip said I was the most alive person he knew. Said he only thought he knew life before he met me. I told him I am a child of grace, that if what he says is true it is only because I have been multiple times killed and resurrected. That I know how little I am, and what I am incapable of.

Danny, on this your 21ˢᵗ birthday, I say to you, brimful of joy, and of peace that came unnaturally born and from no strength of mine—this day I say, God is good. This is what I have to give you.

Aug 6, 2002 *Mama leaves tomorrow after the sunrise. I will take care of myself once she has gone. I will be self-controlled, do only what will bring health: rest, eat what I know I can handle and no more. Papa, these two things sound so simple. But knowing myself I beg Your aid in accomplishing them.*

Next semester I will be these things: humbled, diminished, restrained, dead, laid bare. Truly alive. I will move into new depths of living with grace.

Forgive me, reader, if ever you exist. The pinches from my thoughts that make it to ink are not always consistent.

Aug 2002 *The life I live now is an extra life. Someday, I will learn to sing. Someday I will learn to dance. Until then, I sing. Until then, I dance. I am still that little girl in Europe, disappearing, needing to wander alone. I miss You, Kyrios [Lord]. Revive my heart, wash clean* *my mind with Your truth. Come to me and speak Your secrets, Your plans. Draw me in. I will lay my head on my pillow now and wait.*

Aug 2002 *As I watch my friends my eyes call out to them a Yes! Rejoice, rejoice in your youth! I know what it is like; I have been well and strong too.*

By the time fall semester started, Karis was well enough that even her closest friends, for a while, did not know how much she was struggling.

Hospital silliness

CHAPTER 11

She Was the Princess

Ages Nineteen and Twenty
August 2002-August 2003
Notre Dame Sophomore

"Hey Karis!"

"Karis, my love!"

"Karis, want to meet for lunch?"

"Karis, I read that poem you told me about—awesome!"

"Karis, call me!"

Crossing campus with Karis during her sophomore year was memorable. Everyone seemed to know her, from former President Hesburgh to the workmen cleaning the sidewalk. I mentioned this to Anthony. He grinned and said, "Yeah, I figure that between us we know 75 percent of the people on this campus!"

Leaving her São Paulo friends had been hard, but Karis collected friends at ND as avidly as she had in Brazil. The Black Gospel community, the Asian and Arab communities, the Brazilians and Latin Americans and even the football players claimed her (for tutoring support). She was part of a French conversation group, and participated in two student-led Christian worship groups.

"How do you ever study?" I wondered on one of my visits.

"Oh, I hide!" she giggled. "I have hiding places in the library and the staff people on those floors have sworn on the Bible not to tell anyone when I'm there."

After Karis broke up with Philip, having decided he was not her "Amado," she called me. "Mom, I have a serious problem. I made a list of sevent-five people I think will be hurt if I don't tell them first. What shall I do?"

A few weeks into the semester, Karis began dating Anthony. His reflections tell the story:

The first time I met Karis, I was fascinated as I looked down into those blue eyes looking me straight in the eye as we talked. Unabashed, confident, she seemed to be taking me all in with those smiling eyes. Newly arrived in the US, I was trying to figure out how to fit in and looking for an ally with whom I could share this process. But that evening Karis did not seem concerned with trying to fit in. She was free and relaxed, getting to know other freshman Brazilians.

I got to know Karis better in the honors program. We shared several classes and often ate lunch with students from the program. Karis had an insatiable curiosity. She actually wanted to know, to wrestle deeply with the Truth of things and allow herself to be changed.

Among our numerous Catholic classmates were many truly believing and practicing their faith. Karis became good friends with them and told me about their faith and their way of viewing the world. She was willing to take an honest look at the questions and not accept easy answers.

Karis was a deep thinker. She thought with all of herself, putting her emotions and intuition into the mix. Whenever I asked Karis what she thought about a certain idea or position, she would pause, taking her time, very careful about her choice of words. During our sophomore year, a theology professor told Karis he had never read a paper so profound and so orthodox at the same time.

Karis was primarily geared towards knowing people. It was like she savored them, understanding but not judging them. She was capable of caring deeply about every single one of her friends. And every person she met became her friend. So she was capable of a lot of caring.

When we began dating our sophomore year, I had no idea how Karis was able to make so much time and energy for others. I enjoyed it immensely. I myself am a very social, out-going person. But there were moments when I would just sit back and enjoy watching Karis be Karis, observing how she could connect with all types of people and draw out aspects of them I had never seen before. I enjoyed introducing her to friends and family, seeing how she loved them and how they responded to her.

Karis did not seem to know how to love "half-way." She gave all of herself. She told me a story that I treasured because it helped me understand her. On a class trip her senior year of high school she and her classmates were on some high rocks. In the river below, certain places were deep and others shallow because of large boulders. Nobody quite had the courage to jump. So Karis stepped up and without thinking twice just jumped.

"I figured if I was supposed to die I already would have died several times over," she told me. "So there was nothing really to be afraid of."

All this time, though Karis did all in her power to ignore them, her intestinal symptoms were worsening. A central line and TPN gave her a new lease on life. The health center set aside a room just for her, where she kept her medical supplies and sometimes spent the night for supplementary hydration.

I wore worry like a second skin.

One night, I had already gone to bed in São Paulo when the phone rang. Dr. B, her South Bend physician, said, "I'm very sorry, but I don't think I can be Karis's doctor any longer."

Karis had been found unconscious in her dorm, from simple dehydration. "She *knows* the symptoms," Dr. B lamented. "If she won't do her part, letting me know she needs help, how can I care for her? It's unfair for her to ignore her body and then expect me to bail her out. I've tried to talk to her but she doesn't seem to understand the gravity of the responsibility she expects me to carry."

Dr. B explained that every episode like this caused further damage to Karis's intestine. She *had* to pay attention and call him when she was *starting* to get into trouble, not after she was already in crisis. His case was reasonable, and I presented it to Karis as clearly as I could.

Karis responded, "Well then, I guess you want me to quit college. Mom, here's the thing: I can either pay attention to my body, OR I can have a life. If I pay attention to my symptoms, I won't even get out of bed in the morning. The pain is pretty bad, Mom. I can't let it incapacitate me. Dr. B feels too responsible. Should I sign a statement saying I take responsibility for my own life and choices, and if I die at least I die happy, doing what I want to do?"

We finally settled on some objective criteria Karis couldn't help noticing, like having to leave class or another activity to deal with her diarrhea. She agreed in that case to go by the health center to have them help her decide whether she needed to call Dr. B.

By phone, Dr. B also asked Dave and me to move to South Bend to give Karis support through her remaining college years. I'm not sure who more quickly rejected that request. Karis wanted independence from us. For Dave, Dr. B's idea required such a paradigm shift he didn't entertain it seriously. Our work in Brazil was our life. If Karis couldn't handle college, she should come home.

Coming home was nowhere on Karis's radar. Having "fried the fish" of her doctor dream, Karis evaluated the 75 majors available at Notre Dame. Not satisfied with any of them, she decided to design her own course of study, becoming one of only a few in ND's history to do so.

Karis's hope had been to care for people who suffered from AIDS, especially African female and child victims. Still passionate about helping them, Karis decided to study everything that might fit her to advocate for the needs of women and children in sub-Saharan Africa. She studied history, anthropology, economics, politics, health and social difficulties, French and Arabic, African religions, Islam and the Qur'an, current events, conflicts and conquests and challenges . . .

For her honors thesis, Karis chose to investigate whether the Qur'an could be interpreted as supporting women's rights as defined by the United Nations Universal Declaration of Human Rights. This topic required her to take graduate classes in Islamic schools of law and Qur'anic interpretation.

Soon, though, Karis's own challenges grew even more complex.

> **Oct 16, 2002** *The impossible has happened, has reached in and damaged me on the inside. I don't see a way out of this. I see a long, difficult struggle. I see hurting and baffling those who love me most. But I have no doubt You WILL lead me out of this.*
>
> *Depression. An unknown enemy. I try as I write to tell myself to stop crying. I know what it is now to be truly afraid. My soul is sore where I did not know I had muscle.*
>
>> *She was the princess,*
>> *she was the clean smell*
>> *of sunlight and earth and*
>> *wash out of the dryer; she was*
>> *unafraid of the dog: it would*
>> *yield to her enchantment.*
>> *It didn't. It bit.*

Karis spent fall break in a South Bend hospital, fighting a central line infection. It was an opportunity to discover how Anthony would react to the reality of her compromised health.

> **Oct 18, 2002** *Anthony investigated, unafraid, the needle, the tape, the plastic and tube in my arm—and leaning down, eyes closing in reverence, kissed it. Held my whole arm, elbow and palm; "Karis, there is so much I wish I could spare you . . ." He ran me around the halls to the green elevators in a wheelchair I didn't need. He read aloud to me, such a light in his eyes.*
>
>> *Did I ever love before, Anthony?*
>> *I don't recall ever loving before . . .*
>> *Father, Holy Father*

my "Amado está guardado."
I am consumed . . .
I am enchanted by this your gift.
Let it not be a stumbling block for me.
Lord, be alone enthroned in my heart.

Oct 20, 2002 Lord's Day *Anthony, today we are nineteen and we can do anything we set our minds to. Tomorrow will be more difficult. We both know that.*

I want to be an agent for the healing and purification of Your Bride, Lord. Your Church.

Nov 3, 2002 Lord's Day *All-glad for today. For the worship You threaded through the needle of me.*

Nov 2002 *Learning oneself as an exception—one who has a chronic disease in a competitive university—is much like learning a new language. One must be corrected, held to proper grammar, yet with grace forgive oneself. Thanks to Vera, shoulder-holding my tears, I have that freedom again.*

Dec 2002 *Anthony and I speak, our conversation encompassing whole worlds, past and future, not only of ideas, events, people, but concrete places. We describe ourselves better to each other in speaking of the dust in Turkey or a girl from Ethiopia, than when we begin our sentences, "I . . ."*

Our talk is inefficient, absolutely. Perhaps because no matter what intrigue or pain we delve into, no matter what dead dream, what fear—our every other phrase is always, "But we are together now."

Anthony, you asked me once what I smile at, alone, so often, so always, why every waking moment is joy. When Gustavo asked me I pulled out my hair band and twisted it into a sideways eight. "This is why," I whispered. "Infinity." Because I am with Him always, and He whispers His secrets, and everywhere the thrill of connections, and everywhere His jokes (they are often people).

Because we are together, my Lover and I. And He is different from you, Anthony. He is Lord of all this. I am not afraid of anything but Him, and His enemy who destroys the Beloved, and myself.

And I too often mute, need you, Anthony. You in everything I am not; you in the Plan if you are indeed the one I think you are. If not it will tear my heart out. I was very alone for a very long time, Anthony. "But we are together now." Yes. The three of us. Joy.

Dec 10, 2002 Back in the hospital *God will not take me, as long as He can use me here.*

A few days before Christmas, the distraught tone of Dr. B's voice on the phone registered before my mind caught his message: "I can't let Karis go. She won't survive the trip. She'll dehydrate. . . ."

Karis had been hospitalized on IV's since losing her central line to an infection. After Dr. B hung up, I called Karis and heard her distressed *"NO!! I am not staying here for Christmas! I'm coming home!!"*

Next call: her doctor in Brazil. "That's easy," Dr. G said. "Let her travel with IV's, two of them in case one blows. When she lands in São Paulo, drive her straight to the hospital. I'll meet you there."

Back to Dr. B. He agreed to try, but time was tight. Frantically, the medical team in South Bend hunted for usable veins while an ND campus officer stood by to whisk Karis to the airport.

Twenty hours later in the São Paulo airport, Karis exclaimed, "Everything worked out perfectly! My second IV only blew when we were landing. Can we please go home instead of to the hospital?" NO.

At Einstein Hospital another set of nurses struggled vainly to start one more IV. Dr. G ordered immediate insertion of a central line. Two days later, December 23, surgeon Dr. A still had not located a single catheter in São Paulo or Brazil of the kind Karis needed. "Find a catheter in the US and have it mailed today," he told me. "Karis is running out of time."

I phoned every doctor, hospital, and medical supply store I knew. Nothing. *Hospital policy. Holidays. Stores already closed. . . .* Beside me struggled my daughter: vomiting, non-stop diarrhea; dehydrating. Dan arrived from Yale and slumped in a chair beside his sister's bed, sleeping off end-of-semester fatigue. He roused long enough to mumble, "Call Aunt Karen."

What? Trouble a busy pastor's wife, mother of four, just before Christmas? "Call her," my son insisted.

Karen was quiet for a moment. "This morning I realized I could not do all that was before me today. As I prayed, God told me to set all that aside, because he had another plan for me. I'll call you back."

Intrigued, a little bit hopeful, bereft of other ideas, we waited. How familiar, this posture: nothing more to do but wait on God.

Hours later, the phone rang. Not Karen. A surgeon from Philadelphia, confirming the size and type of catheter Karis needed and the best way to send it. FEDEX only promised delivery December 26. Dr. A reserved an operating room for early morning of December 27. Would the catheter arrive? Could Karis survive four more days?

That evening Karen called back and told us her story. The Philly surgeon had visited their church the previous Sunday. When she was able to track him down, he was delighted to help. "I have several of those very catheters on a storage shelf just a few feet from me," he said. "I'll mail one on my break."

Karis moved in and out of consciousness. On Christmas morning, they got an IV into her foot. A reprieve.

Late on December 26, a FEDEX deliveryman handed me not one, but two packages! Some days later we learned that a medical supply person in Indiana who had told us "no," later had second thoughts. He had returned to his closed store for a catheter, and mailed it to us!

Dec 26, 2002 *It is the night after the night before. Christmas past, the Incarnation. The horrid pain, the black, flat on the bed, inaudible scream. Mother's fear, tubes, beeps, buttons, exhaustion. Incarnation is no respecter of days. This body decaying, scarred, frustrated in the midst of its becoming. Tomorrow it will perhaps be eternally gone. Lord, I surrender my body to tomorrow. They call it sleep. Night before hope: surgery with the rising sun.*

Early December 27, Dr. A. walked into Karis's hospital room looking troubled. A seventeen-year-old's intestine had twisted and died. Cristian needed the same catheter as Karis—not to be found in Brazil. Reverently, I handed Dr. A both FEDEX packages: *two* expensive, life-saving catheters; Christmas gifts straight from heaven (via Philly and South Bend) for Karis *and* for Cristian. For both of them, a new lease on life.

Back at Notre Dame:

Mar 6, 2003 Hospital [After Karis was again found passed out in the dorm] *Strange coming back to the world. I did what I never thought possible with Anthony: I cried. He said "We cannot despair." And gently brought me back, on this small buoy in the ocean.*

Later *Mama arrived. Long night of pain. My body's not well but the problem is my lack of "WILL." I'm trying to collect the strands of my life and re-weave them but I hate what I see. A life badly put together, sloppy. I have no pride in myself. I want to come back to life but I need help. I traveled on roads beyond this world—I got lost there. My body brought me back through no choice of my own. Papa, I hate self-pity, sentimentality and weakness of spirit. I am ashamed. I wish I could begin again.*

But I do begin again multiple times a day and don't You tire of me? I tire of me. Spoiled brat.

Lord, it will do neither of us good to begin a tirade against this Your creature, Your Beloved Child, myself. But how I hate the way my mother has found me! And what ability I do have, to think, cope, continue, only shames me further. Invisible manacles. Would that I were fully incapacitated or not at all. This hinterland forces words to be lies, no matter the words. Help me.

Later *I will thank You. Yes. Worship and wait. For hundreds of loving arms, offers to help—I thank You. (And in thanking must accept the gift, yes?) I try. Accepting is hard. Facing myself is difficult.*

Rest and psalms. Prayer. Sleep. Love. Restoration. Rest-oration. Only because He is Emmanuel.

I have given up on writing more than fragments.

Later *Anthony said the answers to some of my questions only I could discover; that I force him to wrestle with God. My decisions were beyond "right and wrong." Perhaps yes. But not beyond good and evil? I told him I do not begrudge the way things are, know and am glad God is working according to His right over my life. I only fear I will not stand up under it.*

He said, good place we all should reach: that we cannot, and need Him. Thoroughly and yes, desperately. Thank You that he is not afraid of this dark night of my soul.

Anthony wrote:

One of the hardest things for me was to see Karis in pain. Someone who did not know her would not have been able to tell; she did not show many outward signs. She was slightly distracted, and would take an extra few seconds to respond to you, or ask you to repeat yourself. I began to see this side of her more our sophomore year. It was strange because I had never known Karis to be sick. She had told me about her situation but I had always known her as this incredibly energetic healthy person. At times she would get this glazed look and have a hard time responding and interacting. It felt somehow like she had gone away, like she wasn't quite Karis.

Mar 18, 2003 Still in the hospital *I am amazed. By a body's capacity. For pain.*

Forcing my arms to hang limp, forcing my fists to keep innocuously from the walls where they would surely splinter the plastic colored railings, and the hall-peace, I plod. Wanting each time I pass my door to leave my brown wet shrivel-petal ghost of a self gently on the bed to rest. Moving on in driven pain, in the shooting high-pitched blue of neck, stomach, only this me still moving.

But now, tide is down enough, just as I begged You, down enough to gather the nerve-endings and clusters of thoughts, into my finger-grooves, taut enough, and begin again to weave.

I am amazed.

By a body's capacity.

For pain.

What have You planted and watered this long at the soul of my heart; what is this I would fight you for? It is my Beloved ones: Greg, and Robin, and Becca.

There is (I say this almost with the self-horror of a heretic) a way in which You left me, turned Your back on me. For a time, yes? This is my stepping out. My faith that You do not need me to defend You and do not want me to bend always prostrate. Though I could—by Your majesty—gladly would.

I told Anthony maybe You will destroy my fear of myself in this, showing me what I can stand up under. But I risk that I might later hate and hurt Your Church which is my heart; or lose Anthony's love; or grieve my parents. Be ruined for life or lose my own soul. But I must come here. To You. For once in my life with clenched fists. For this first time in my life.

Mar 25, 2003 Back on campus *In class we are observing how fortunate we are to have the ability to forget.*

Apr 2, 2003 *Last night I dared share with Anthony my trembling dream of writing like Barbara Kingsolver or Anne de Graaf, international, intimate. My dream of capturing joy in my poems as powerfully as my whole cloud of witnesses, each author with whom I have communed. As powerfully as men for centuries have given vulnerable pain,* **I want to give joy**. *Visceral.*

Apr 2003 *Karis. Grace. I argued, laughing with Hannah about whether my name really means grace or gift. Utterly silly. And the Lord sent my grandfather to me, over the phone, speaking words of encouragement straight to my turmoil. PopPop said Gift. That Dad was stepping out of bounds somehow in giving me that name. That when PopPop heard it, there was a block in his spirit. He was afraid God would—he knew God would—test my father, challenge him on that name. So Lord, did my parents call into being this creature Karis, by naming her? The gift of my life—oh, Mama, how you have fought for it! How you have taken all the messy means of medicine upon yourself and given up your own living often to keep this gift!*

May I also cling to, grapple for, the gifts I have been given. May I learn to fight for my faith. For my love. For Your continued ear and strong arm working through me, Lord. Teach me to treasure Your gifts. Not ever above Your own Being, but still to guard them, loving as best I know how.

Apr 10, 2003 *I imagined myself and Anthony, a Clare and Francis, chaste in love. I laughed but could imagine it. I dance, mother to none. But one day my daughter will sing, vibrate all of the heavens, draw Spirit into her lungs . . . and she will have twirly skirts.*

Apr 2003 *Of all Earth I am this night most to be envied. Trying and not succeeding at ugliness. My body—puffy, pained, tummy distended like pregnancy—is free, free, free. Do you see the tears of this joy? Had I been beautiful I would perhaps never have realized how Anthony loves me.*

Apr 2003 *Oh you silly, who cannot finish a paper.*

But I want you to know, professors, how I walk: though failing the law, in step with the spirit; though I don't meet deadlines I arduously and joyously (no exaggeration) weave together the life lines of thought. I want you to know I have heard you.

Apr 20, 2003 *Anthony breathed enough life into me to bring me here to You, reminding me You demand no more than all I have to give.*

In May, Karis and Anthony joined our family in New Haven to celebrate Dan's graduation from Yale and wish him well in his new job in New York City. Anthony then traveled to Europe and Karis to Brazil. Karis had many ambitions for the summer, especially to research options for improving Brazil's libraries. Her health, though, kept her on the couch more often than out in São Paulo's streets.

Jun 14, 2003 *Lord, You asked me: "What do you want?" I want to be an intercessor: to hear Your heart for people and return it to You as I have in the past. I want to be healed. Yet, You have again confirmed to me, "No, but my grace is sufficient." Father, let me SEE what You are doing in my life.*

*You said to me "**Seu amado está guardado**." And so he is. Only prepare me, Lord, for Anthony. You said to me "**You will be a door for the nations**." Renew in me my passion for Your Gospel . . . and in Your time, give me the promised key.*

Dave's letter to Karis at the end of the summer reflects the challenges of her weeks at home:

This has been such a hard summer in many ways. As we head into your junior year, Sweetheart, I want you to raise your head with eyes of faith. Isaiah 40:27-30: "He gives power to the weak . . ." Karis, you arrived worn out and you're leaving worn out. It's been hard to be so often feverish and bed-ridden; hard to realize that in your present state you can't possibly tackle the challenges of this next semester at ND. May God lift you up. I believe this is a special word from God letting you know that as you wait on Him, God will be working on your behalf to raise you up for this next semester. I love you, Dad

Fall semester at Notre Dame

CHAPTER 12

Make My Life Sacrament

Ages Twenty and Twenty-One
August 2003-August 2004
Notre Dame, Pittsburgh, Istanbul

After her difficult summer in São Paulo, Dave and I questioned whether Karis was well enough to return to school. She appealed to her old mantras, "I may never be better than this," and "How will I know if I don't try?"

Rachel, Karis, and I traveled to the US together, so I could accompany Rachel to her freshman orientation at Wheaton College. Dan was working in New York City, leaving only Valerie still at home in São Paulo. Returning to Notre Dame, Karis missed Anthony terribly, and wondered whether their relationship could sustain a year-long separation while he studied in Germany and Austria.

Back home in São Paulo, a friend sent us an article about intestinal transplantation. The concept sent shock waves through my soul. Something had to be done to help Karis—but *this*?!

Years before, Dr. P had told me not to pay attention to rumors of intestinal transplant. The very thought terrified me. But we had to face Karis's lack of venous access for TPN. She was entirely dependent now on IV nutrition; without it, she would starve, or die from dehydration. Intestinal transplant required two central lines, and it wasn't clear to us that she could maintain even one. Our son Dan made us acknowledge the paucity of Karis's options.

At the end of September, Karis was hospitalized with her sixth line infection of the year. Once more, I traveled to South Bend to sit at her bedside while she fought for her life. When she was better, I told her what we had learned about intestinal transplant.

Karis decided it was worth at least learning more, and we were able to schedule a transplant evaluation for her in November in Pittsburgh. Dave and I flew there from Brazil, Dan from New York, my sister Jan from Mexico, and Karis from South Bend. While Karis underwent comprehensive medical evaluation, we all took a class called "The Good, the Bad, and the Ugly of Intestinal Transplantation."

As part of the evaluation, we were assessed as a family to determine whether we could offer Karis enough support for her to make it through at least six months of recuperation post-surgery. One of us must become Karis's main caregiver and point person for communication with medical personnel. That person—me—would be expected to accompany every part of Karis's drama through the transplant itself and her convalescence.

In every dimension, intestinal transplant is more complex than transplant of "solid" organs like the heart or kidneys or liver. In 2003, it was still on trial as a viable solution to intestinal failure. Only that year had insurance companies approved payment for the surgery. But the trend was encouraging. In 2002 patients had 77% chance of survival for one year and 51% for five years,[9] but new immunotherapy protocols were having a positive effect. In 2003 Pittsburgh could boast 81% survival at one year.[10]

Because of the fragility of Karis's veins, the transplant team wanted to put her immediately at the top of the waiting list for an intestine. Her response was an emphatic NO. Anthony, who had been studying in Europe the past semester, had invited her to Turkey for Christmas with his family! Risky and complicated as it might be, she was determined to go. When Dan offered to accompany her, the decision was made. She would be listed for transplant upon their return from Turkey in January. First, though, Karis had to finish her semester at ND.

> **Dec 12, 2003** *Friday I broke. My doctor later wrote to my mother, "She cried—you know she doesn't <u>do</u> that." And I don't. I never have before, not with a doctor. It shocked me, took me over against my will. Since then I've stayed broken. Whether I ignore it and work, give leeway to it and sob; whether I sing Christmas carols at the top of my lungs; whether I confess it to friends and allow them to hug me and pray for me, or toss my head back and laugh and say I'm fine and concern myself with <u>their</u> concerns—none of these things touch it.*

---

[9] http://onlinelibrary.wiley.com/doi/10.1034/j.1600-6143.3.s4.8.x/full
[10] https://www.ncbi.nlm.nih.gov/pubmed/15798462

The gestures of my soul are bound
never to exceed the traced intention . . .
Why so bewildered my soul? Why troubled?
How now that your throes
of agony can overcome my mind,
though it in peace still claims to abide? . . .

I am a train derailed.

The fascinating thing is that I find myself now in a place common to
all men. I wake up hating the day. I know this is a common experience
(though not common to me). Then, looking at my work, I am utterly
uninterested in it. Isn't this also normal for many people?

Karis ended the semester with two incompletes. And though Anthony's family warmly welcomed Karis and Dan, and Istanbul enchanted them, the visit soon grew bittersweet. Karis had not seen Anthony for eight months. She discovered that he was changing in critical ways, including his feelings toward her. He had met a young woman through his study program in Austria who believed God had called her to guide him into Catholicism, and they had grown close.

Dec 2003 *Since Christmas Eve I have been living a new life. Filled, yes,*
with the ebony, jade, mother-of-pearl of Topkapi Palace; the enduring
mystique of the Hagia Sophia. Lattices, goblets, domes, tiles. The salt
of the Bosphorus and lingering mint steam from the water pipes we
smoked. Tea and orchid root with cinnamon. The ferry, my brother's
arm around me as I stared out over the water.

All of this has faded with the realization that comes to me from Anthony:
my focus was all off. I had been living a half-life, more concerned with
my immediate needs than with the mind of Christ. He showed me the
Lord's care for me has not flagged. His Word, like manna, has to be
daily. Meditation and prayer, drawing into the Father's presence and
hearing His voice, must be my survival.

I told Anthony I have no expectations. When has anyone ever given me a promise about the future? My days in Istanbul are numbered. Dehydrated, I must waste one of them with a trip to the hospital.

New Year's Day *This realization has become important in my thinking: the Lord wounds, but He also binds up. His work in us is not merely healing and restoring. His work comes also in wounding.*

Upon my return the bulk of the semester's work awaits me. The Africa paper. Iraq and pacifism, both of which have turned to ashes in my mouth. But set that aside, worries for another day. I come into Your Presence, Lord, praying, praying You would draw me to the fountain of Living Water, the Life that will make this new year possible, not within myself—how bleak my spirit, my prospects!—but here, in You.

*Looking back on this time with Anthony, I realize I had let my relationship with him take a place in my heart and mind and body that was not due it. **I am not a garden but rather a sacked city**. That said, my body remembers its hope is in the Lord and knows content in itself. I worship You, Lord, for making me for Yourself. I worship You for drawing me in these days to wholeness and freedom. **My body will live in hope** [Psalm 43:5].*

*My body has been living in the absence of hope. **To live in hope is not to be a victim**. To live in hope is the premise of God's abundance rather than apparent scarcity, thus to have plenty and no need to grasp. To live in hope is to smile in the midst of false hunger or desire, to know my needs are met and I have been blessed. To know His grace is sufficient.*

Jan 5, 2003 *I feel a divorce between Anthony's mind and mine, the distance between our thoughts. I want a companion. I am going into transplant now and no matter how solicitous and concerned Anthony has been, I feel as though I am entering it alone.*

This is not ME, but in this moment: I need. Why do I not articulate that to him? Because I am afraid now. Because he is Evaluating. I don't want the Evaluation to be a way in which he receives my gestures. I don't want him to conclude from each weakness or strength, "this is who she is," and then ask, "do I love her?" No amount of positive things he can say about me can make me happier. They don't touch me. They are observations. Compliments. Attempts to be kind, to build me up.

No, I don't need you to tell me I'm beautiful, Anthony. I don't need you to prop up my self-esteem. I don't need to care whether or not I'm good enough for you. I need to be like a sister. I need someone with whom to seek God. I need someone to look this year in the face and cry with me.

But he doesn't see how much I need simply to be enjoyed, simply to share the joy there is in living.

Karis hooked herself up to TPN before leaving with Dan for the Istanbul airport for their return trip. At check-in, airline personnel saw the plastic tube emerging from her TPN backpack into her body, heard her mini-pump softly audible as it counted down the minutes remaining on the infusion, and thought she was a suicide bomber! Turkish police took Karis by herself into a room where they stripped and interrogated her. They kept her for so many hours that Dan was frantic. He had no idea what was happening to his sister, fearing the police might even pull out the central line and confiscate her pump.

Somehow, praise God, the police eventually believed Karis was not dangerous. Rerouted through Germany, where they encountered a few more hiccups, Karis and Dan finally arrived safely back in the United States. Her exhaustion from the ordeal, combined with intensely cold winter weather, meant she spent the rest of her break inside and in bed rather than out having the adventures she had planned.

Jan 6, 2004 USA again *I don't even know what to say of my feelings about Anthony. To delve into them seems futile. I have to call Mom and Dad soon. What shall I say? Before I speak with them, Lord, take my tears. Be my comforter and make me steadfast. Lord, I come fainting from hunger and hoping for daily bread.*

Jan 7, 2004 *I just received an email from Anthony, and was amazed at the hostility it engendered in me—almost like my own body, something I hate but cannot repudiate. More and more it is dawning on me to feel like a fool. I made a fool of myself. Constantly, in the first few days in Istanbul, I wanted to be with him. Consistently and kindly he repudiated me. In the end, there was almost nothing to be said. How many times it was on my lips to ask him if he didn't just want to break up.*

It does no good to fret over this. Ambiguity, the not-knowing-of-the-other: don't most people deal with this daily? But for me this is the first time I have set myself up for core rejection, the first time I have sighted it on the horizon and even suspected it is already upon me.

To believe someone's love for me could actually hinge on my behavior twists my insides. Lord, what can I do with this? Is it right to tell Anthony any of my jumbled feelings? This crucible . . . is it possible to escape it and still love? Or to survive it and still be intact, myself?

Jan 2004 *As I begin this new semester, when I dance, Lord, may I dance before You, for the pleasure of Your eyes, for pure child joy, for the fullness rather than the degradation of Your creation. In pain may I worship rather than wilt. May my pain over Anthony serve for building up my friends. As I sobbed in thanks last night, thank You for soon bringing Mama to be with me.*

Lord, forgive me for indulging too much, taking too much from my relationship with Anthony. I should have invested so much of that time in others who need You. Forgive me.

The new semester at Notre Dame began for Karis with the two incompletes hanging over her head and a number of items still to check off the transplant-preparation list, including hospitalization for removal of her wisdom teeth. Before transplant, every possible or potential medical or dental concern had to be treated. This did not help her progress in her classes at ND.

Jan 12, 2004 *As one who does not know her own name but is content to know it is engraved on Your hand; as one buried in Your bosom, whose thoughts are heard even before I utter them; as a woman who knows "**meu amado está guardado**" and whose body is learning to live in hope, not for man but for God—I deliver to You the loose ends of my soul.*

The other day I caught a glance of myself in the mirror and was struck by the fact that I am an eternal being. That awareness made ludicrous the continuous sense of having been disheveled by the moment, the chains which tug one again and again to pause before the glass and adjust. They are powerful, these currents which keep one checking, wondering, fretting.

But the girl there is an eternal being. Her constantly fluctuating body will be there in eternity; and more glorious then than now. I get this itching, tickling hope, full of mirth and expectation. Soon, perhaps, it will of its own accord be flowing through my soul.

Jan 2004 *I've been thinking of Anthony and me, and play. Children develop largely through play. Anthony and I—our relationship—needs a longer childhood. This is what I have been trying to articulate for nigh on a month now. Let us play. Let us explore. Let us make mistakes and hold each other lightly.*

Isn't the extent to which my parents were capable of carelessness my glory? That they sent me off to college? To Turkey? That they let me ride the horses, the waves . . . doesn't true confidence come from facing the world raw? Show me how small and stretched I am. One day, Father, will I grow up?

It is the hour you love most, Anthony: the sun almost sets, tinging the snow soft blue. There are no shadows and yet all is shadow; there is no darkness, only this constancy in the air. One could fall in love with a warthog.

Though Karis realized her relationship with Anthony had changed, their breakup in early February devastated her. Much of her subsequent journaling addresses her intense grieving of her "Amado" and best friend, just when she was facing the most frightening prospect of her life: intestinal transplant. Most of what she journaled is too personal to share. Karis expressed more agony over loss of the friendship she so treasured with Anthony than loss of the romance. She felt betrayed. She felt abandoned.

Feb 2004 *Just got off the phone with Anthony. Anger. Frustrated tears. He told me to be angry, to let out my—I said I didn't know how.*

But inside I scream and scream as if he had me on a spit turning. Every time he tells me he doesn't love me it is almost a physical stab, surprising no matter how I try to anticipate it. There are no words, there is no vocabulary. There is utter void.

So this is what it is like. To be rejected. To be dropped. To be unloved. To die inside. It is a human experience; they sing about it every day on the radio. I've fielded dozens of sobbing, raging people who have gone through this. Perhaps everyone but me already has.

God it's all so stupid! God, I'm such a . . . a . . . everything I shake my head at—to hope every few minutes again that he will have repented, that he will return and there will be an e-mail from him—or a voice filled half with awe and hope and joy—and half with the greatest pain, and shame—that he'll realize how much he loves me and how I've hurt . . .

Oh, God, who strung my nose and when, to make a puppet of me now?

As if each moment were a bump, my heart jolts over it. Who have I become? That my patience and my joy are just—gone? Out of reach? That I woke today and even the thought of dressing was overwhelming?! It is not only a physical malady, Lord. They say let your anger out. But say what, to whom? If only I could merely explode, in the loudest of odorless pops.

I want Vera! I want Mama, I want Rachel— [Her friend Vera was studying abroad this semester.]

I arrived in South Bend February 6, knowing that Karis could be called for transplant any time. I had to buy cell phones for both Karis and me—our first!—so that we could be reached any time day or night should an intestine become available for Karis. We would then have four hours to arrive at the hospital in Pittsburgh. The unpredictability made it impossible to schedule a flight. I researched a list of private pilots who might be able to take us to Pittsburgh when the time came.

Karis resented having a cell phone! She wanted always to be fully present to the person before her at any given moment. She didn't want to be part of the cell phone culture, where people talked on their phones at the expense of those around them. But she had no choice. She had to be available at any moment to respond to a call for transplant.

Overwhelmed by the prospect of major surgery and by the breakup with Anthony, along with her daily struggle with pain and dehydration, Karis rarely went to classes and hardly did any of her work. She spent much of her time resting, trying to muster energy to help me sort and pack her things. Her dean and dorm director understood that this would be a lost semester for her. Notre Dame's willingness to tolerate this situation so generously is part of the huge debt of love we owe to the university.

The first transplant call came as a shock shortly after I arrived in South Bend. Blood drained from Karis's face as she listened to the voice on her new cell phone; then she threw the phone to me, saying, "Mama, tell them no!"

It was a wake-up call: suddenly the idea of transplant took on the terrifying aspect of reality. Karis had to decide whether she really wanted to go through with it. Intestinal transplant offered a hope—a slim hope—for extending her life and an even slimmer hope of restoring sufficient quality of life to pursue her dreams and plans, but the prospect of actually *doing* it paralyzed her.

Mar 9, 2004 *When I am weak, then I am strong You say? So where, in this moment, is this strength You speak of? I have gathered the silence of*

many hours into the strength to compose and record these simple words.
I have as yet no energy for emotion. I have become self-absorbed, mute.

Just before midnight on Friday, March 27, Karis received a second transplant call. This time she was ready to say yes. We flew to Pittsburgh by private jet and she was immediately prepped for surgery—only to have the transplant cancelled!

Whiplash.

Two days later Kars was called again, and once more the surgery was cancelled. Having moved lock, stock, and barrel to Pittsburgh, we decided to stay there while we awaited another call. After receiving these two calls back to back, we thought another would come soon, but it was not to be. From the end of March until mid-August, no more transplant calls came.

For all that time, we lived in limbo in a strange city, our ears constantly tuned to our cell phones. For five months we waited, wondering whether we were in the right place doing the right thing. I had expected to have returned to Brazil and Karis to Notre Dame, *post*-transplant and recovery, by the time the real transplant call finally came.

In hindsight, we discerned a variety of benefits from those surreal five months of "down time":

- We learned to navigate Pittsburgh. Every day that Karis felt well enough, we went somewhere, randomly exploring a neighborhood or one of many nearby state parks. We enjoyed museums and concerts, art shows and Pirates games. Inevitably we got lost trying to find our way up and down and over and around this charming, hilly, three-rivers-and-many-bridges city. We didn't have our own car, but found various ways to get around.

- We met people and made friends, with no idea how invaluable this would be for what lay ahead. We involved ourselves with our new worship community, Church of the Ascension.

- Under the care of Pittsburgh specialists, and without the pressure of school, Karis grew stronger than she had been for years. We even wondered whether she actually needed a transplant. But she still couldn't eat. Her lack of venous access for long-term TPN was still the bottom line.

- Karis was able to finish her incompletes from fall semester. She made friends with Arabic speakers and joined a French club to keep up her fluency in those two languages.

God used Psalm 37 to help me settle down and invest in Pittsburgh, "possessing" this new land. "Trust in the Lord and do good . . . Commit everything you do to the Lord. Trust him, and he will help you . . . Be still and wait patiently for him to act . . . Day by day the Lord takes care . . . Put your hope in the Lord. Travel steadily along his path. . . ."

Still, I struggled with my own sense of identity in Pittsburgh. I was used to an active life of service in Brazil, where I had a niche, a place. In Pittsburgh, I had no identity other than as Karis's mom. I could do some work for Dave remotely, but in Pittsburgh, my Brazilian roles and functions mattered not at all.

I was distressed over the separation from my youngest daughter, Valerie, who had just turned sixteen and was bouncing around among various friends' homes in São Paulo because her father traveled so much. Valerie called herself our "abandoned child." She didn't want to move to Pittsburgh where she knew no one, but she had lost the stable base of our home and family life. She lived with the constant tension of not knowing hour to hour how her beloved sister was faring. Sometimes she didn't have internet access and only learned at school from her teachers what they had read on Karis's prayer blog.

In May, after completing her freshman year at Wheaton College, Rachel decided to work with an inner-city day camp in Pittsburgh for the summer. Though she was so busy we seldom saw her, Karis and I loved having Rachel nearby. Our son Dan visited us from New York. Every couple of months, Dave visited from Brazil.

As this waiting time extended, with no idea when another transplant call would come, the value of "being" rather than doing was pounded into me. I had to learn lessons of trust in God for the care of our scattered family and for all of the people and projects I had left behind in Brazil.

God brought many wonderful new friends into our lives in Pittsburgh, including Brazilians. We shared transplant clinic waiting-room time with families from around the world. Martha, wife of our Ascension small group leader and the recipient of three kidney transplants, understood many of Karis's challenges and encouraged us with her optimism. They shared with us their "little house in the big woods," a place of retreat near Pittsburgh. Karis invested in Three Nails, a gathering of young people who became her core support group, and in Ascension's college group, led by Tina, who walked closely with her.

During this waiting time, Karis wrote:

> **Apr 2004** *Christ himself learned through what he suffered, and through discipline. And even he submitted himself to the limitations of a suffering human body. Should not we?*
>
> *Ask if you must why God does not heal me. But do so looking to find out what he is up to. Challenge Him, wrestle Him, and He will humble you. He will break you and rename you. He will be with you all the night. He is the Mighty One who both wounds and heals. My Hallelujah.*

Karis "celebrated" her twenty-first birthday hospitalized with bowel obstruction.

> **May 2004** *Turning 21, I am plagued by the question, what is maturity? Can one be identified as mature only insofar as one is "ahead" relative to one's peers? Is it a capacity for patience and unselfishness? Or the ability to speak with grace, interacting with those older than oneself?*
>
> *It is hard for me to identify in what capacity I am an adult, while living under my mother's care, having no driver's license or job. I feel*

this fundamental question in many of my interactions with people older than myself: "Am I—okay? Am I doing well enough; do I 'have it together'"?

Jun 2004 *How long the wait, Father? To what extent can I ally myself with the here and now? Pittsburgh, city of bridges. If I build here will I lose myself? Will I become tied to this place?*

Though for a while she dated a young man in Pittsburgh, Karis's grieving for Anthony continued.

I harbor Anthony in my under-skin. Six feet under the surface. I long to learn how to love again. But something in me is stuck on Anthony: and it's he himself, not just a creature with his attributes. I'm not sure I would be capable of loving a man right now even if he played soccer as well, even if he were as reverent, as good with kids, even if he understood my poetry as Anthony never did or loved those I love and was knowledgeable and passionate about art, on top of world events, above me in character and maturity, creative, able to enjoy my family's sense of humor, laughing often—

Jun 26, 2004 *Lord, I'm trying desperately not to implode. You have given me this vast amount of time and expect I will know how to fill it. But Lord, I'm failing. I can draw nothing more out of myself.*

The robust spirit in me is intensely ticked off. Isn't that the spirit I need or the world will crush me? But I don't have it. I'm crushed already. I want always to stay home and rest just one more day and tomorrow I will be well enough. I am paralyzed. Lord, how long since I have known Your Presence? Or my own careless bottomless joy? Have mercy . . .

I'm reading Larry Crabb's "Shattered Dreams." He says, "In every case, when good dreams shatter, better ones are there to newly value and pursue." All I can say to him is, you lie.

Jul 2004 *Give me faith that in breaking me You are engaged in my purification. Teach me to believe I am heard when I cry and this time* *is seen by You, whether by anyone else or not. Yes, Lord. Finally I will **consent to be nothing for a while**. To be alone with You. My Solace. Work in me the Wonderful Life You have planned, despite the constant frustration of the dreams I dreamed for myself. I believe in Your immutability, Lord. It gives me greatest comfort to be incapable of manipulating You.*

I believe I will be a door; that someday** whether or not to my knowledge **there will be a key. And nations will enter Your Presence.

Karis continued this journal entry reviewing her life since arriving at Notre Dame. She went on to discuss economics, Socrates, Hobbes, Jacques Maritain, T.S. Eliot, Pinsky, Rousseau, Andrei Sakharov, and the Qur'an; Proust and Heidegger and various poets. . . . In July 2004, no one could foresee that soon Karis would enter a coma from which she would emerge unable even to read or write or do simple arithmetic.

Jul 20, 2004

> *I awake not only to a lofty God but to an*
> *Unfathomed freedom.*
> *Remember this to me.*
> *Remember me in moving*
> *By Your grace through rather than*
> *Beside. **Make my life Sacrament**.[11]*
> *Turn my gaze toward the subject*
> *Of Your eye.*
>
> *Forgive me that I do not love; forgive*
> *And rush into the lack in me*
> *Teach me to pray*
> *Teach me to wait*
> *Teach me to believe You love me.*

---

[11] Sacrament: An outward and visible sign of inward and spiritual divine grace.

Aug 2004 *My path is hard to justify to strangers. Soon, I fear, it will become impossible to explain to friends. Papa, come with me! You will be the only one to go with me, where I will go.*

Aug 2004 [translated from Portuguese] *People call me heroic for enduring the physical discomfort I live with. But this world is home for none of us. The only true distress is when You hide Yourself from us. It doesn't really matter whether we are physically whole or not.*

Aug 2004 *How sweet it is, after a couple days wading the Qur'an, to fall back into the familiar lucidity of Scripture! I need You, Lord, to help me give better support to my friends. Give me persistence in prayer for them, Lord. Let my thoughts and my words be of real value to them.*

August 14, a transplant opportunity was aborted because Karis was sick. A huge disappointment.

Aug 17, 2004 *Can I cry now? Can I run? No, I can't go out running anymore. But I can cry, yes? Out of shock that despite the weekend of infection, here I still am? Out of frustration because of how starved I am for access to myself? If only I could wail and throw myself about. If only I had been taught outward expressions of grief. To howl. I come to the limits not of my strength but of the rest of myself: patience, empathy, honesty, loyalty, selflessness, humility, joy, peace.*

Aug 2004 *My friends and sisters have gone back to school. Beginning "our" senior year at ND. I mourn. Prematurely I have mourned lost friendships, a lost self. You have humbled me.*

Aug 2004 *"Unless the Lord builds the house, its builders labor in vain" Psalm 127:1-2. Let me build ever so slowly a mind which leans on Yours but is otherwise independent, scaffolded by the wisdom of the likes of C.S. Lewis.*

These were the last words Karis journaled before she finally received "the" call for transplant on August 24.

Christmas 2004 in the ICU
Valerie, Dave, Rachel, Debbie, Dan, Karis

CHAPTER 13

Smiling Like No One Else Can Smile

Age Twenty-One
August 25, 2004-January 2005
Pittsburgh

Notre Dame friend Greg wrote to Karis on Nov 10, 2004:

> What do you write to a friend going through something you can't imagine? How do you thank her for the light she's been in your life? I don't remember the first time we met. I only recall a girl standing in the back of Campus Fellowship meetings smiling . . . **smiling like no one else can smile**. She was so joyful and peaceful, always with time for you. She saw a beauty in you that no one else did. She really did love <u>you</u>. And she loved everyone. It didn't matter if they were cool or smart or nice, she loved everyone, each as a unique son or daughter of God.

> Karis, you amaze me. I don't know anyone who loves like you do. I find myself unable to describe the light you have always been to me. You shine the glory, power, and love of God for all to see. If I have ever seen Christ, I have seen Him in you; in your eyes, in your smile, in your love. If I could move one mountain it would be the one under whose weight you suffer. I hope with every ounce of love in my heart that you might be healed.

This is one of hundreds of cards, letters, and emails kind people sent to Karis and our family the fall of 2004 and spring of 2005, as we were "going through something you can't imagine," in Greg's words.

The transplant and initial recovery went well; Karis even broke records for getting off the ventilator, out of ICU, and going home. She claimed ice chips were "the best thing in the whole world." And soon she could eat anything she wanted!! *For the first time in years, Karis had the experience of eating and not feeling sick from doing so!* For a girl who had depended on being fed through a plastic catheter in her veins, eating a hamburger was an unbelievably exciting moment.

Sep 21, 2004 *It turns out to be a full-time job to recover from this surgery. I hate being famous for being sick. I have a complicated love-hate affair with the much elegized blog that publishes my life to the world. Couldn't I just disappear? But where to, where do the Internet and the interconnected Body of Christ not already know my name and*

my struggle? I've fought my whole life for the right to be a mere "part"
of the world, and not its center. Despite everything, I glow joy.

When asked post-surgery about the condition of Karis's old intestine, Dr. S
exclaimed, "Oh, it was awful! We can't imagine how Karis survived as long
as she did. None of the imaging we did prepared us for the shock of what
her intestine looked like. The pain Karis lived with every day is beyond
imagining. She has a whole new life ahead of her now!"

Friday, September 24, only a month post-transplant, Karis was discharged
from the hospital, thus setting a record. That day we were invited to the
pathology lab to view her old intestine displayed next to a normal one.
Both had been cut open lengthwise. The normal intestine was two inches
wide, soft and velvety like a balloon (a little thicker). Karis's was twice as
wide and as thick and inflexible as an old piece of tire. It was a bit over 3
feet long, one quarter of normal length. The pathologist told us that the
microscope showed *nerves so few, small, scattered, and malformed it seemed*
impossible that her old intestine had ever functioned. These were the same
words we had heard when she was an infant, and again when she was
eleven. Clearly, transplant was the right decision for Karis.

Sep 25, 2004 *Waking up at home is pure delight!!*

Karis's first post-surgery shower was "the best thing in the whole world."
She squealed with pleasure.

Sep 26, 2004 *Thanks to You, Lord. Thanks to miracles of surrender*
and healing, and radical choices to push new medical frontiers. What
*to do, Lord, with **unmerited love** but accept it? **That is what my life***
***has been.** All I can do is return it, knowing at every step that I am the*
debtor in the equation.

We weren't even home from a check-up on Tuesday, September 28,
however, when my cell phone rang. "Bring Karis back to the hospital; the
endoscopy visually looks like rejection and the doctors want her to have a
dose of steroids." Biopsy results confirmed mild-moderate rejection, and
Karis had to be readmitted.

Sep 28, 2004 *It's a beautiful night, despite being back in the hospital. Last night I began to remember who I am. I was honestly surprised by it: I had forgotten what I was doing with my major, and the work with kids; how I used to dance, used to dwell in poetry.*

*I remembered some of the blessed images which inhabit me and can guide my relation to the people I love: the drawing I made for Anthony last November of the woman with her **hair and perfume and self broken over Jesus' feet**; and also the **lessons of the Pantanal**,[12] the water receding, the teeming waters becoming a thousand tiny scaly deaths and the feast of the birds. **Broken and poured out for others**. I nurture hope because **Your grace flows through my weakness**.*

I will be disciplined. As I have been, already, this week. The work of rebuilding myself will be long and labor-intensive. It will involve learning to push people away and say many a "no." But life is so good. I am surrounded by good things to do and swimming in the grace in which to learn them.

On mega-steroids to fight the rejection, Karis was "wired." She had enough energy September 30 to write on her blog: "*Pray for me in the discovery of the 'new me,' with completely different parameters, which will emerge in these next months.*" But this warm optimism didn't last. October 4, Karis was taken back to ICU with "severe" rejection and EBV (the "mono" virus) as well.

"This is a time to strengthen your faith and ask all of your friends to pray for you. We need to fight with more than just medicine." Dr. S's sober words accented the trickiness of wiping out an immune system to treat rejection, because this creates extreme susceptibility to infections. The treatment for these two conditions, rejection and infection, is opposite; we depend on our immune systems to resist and fight infections. Walking

---

[12] In 2003 our family visited the Pantanal, in central-west Brazil, to commemorate Rachel's graduation from PACA. It deeply impacted Karis. She asked before she died to have her ashes scattered in this place where life is continually reborn out of death.

the infection/rejection tightrope is an immense challenge for transplant recipients and their doctors.

Oct-something *I won't stay ugly. I'll grow into some new form of beauty and wellness. Why do I know that? Why do I know I won't die?* **Because there are unfulfilled promises.** *It's so simple when I remember that. Surely my friends recognized Your grace in me, and were enchanted by that. That is when I can enter their lives and touch and interact. That is when the knowledge that I will leave an impact is joyous.*

Oct 19, 2004 *I think life was already good. You could have taken it anywhere. Yet You chose to crush the pot. It was cracked of course— always had been, but with Your own crack, watering flowers—*

Now Your idea is better? To destroy what was? It is beyond me; it boggles my mind. To be this moment of smooshed clay on a silent wheel beneath Your hands.

Oct 20, 2004 *My suffering body is the only thing I have brought through the year, the only thing I really have to give. That and my joy, my faith, my love. I come poor and ashamed of my poverty, but bringing all I have. Gentle and quiet my spirit; may Your Spirit within me shine forth. I want to forget my own desires warring inside me and be freed to serenity. Today. Teach me to be a good friend.*

On "third tier" weaponry against rejection, Karis experienced awful side effects. To summarize an impossibly long miracle story: Karis never conquered the rejection. Her graft (transplanted intestine) had to be removed after she contracted Legionnaire's Disease, a pneumonia not seen in that hospital for twelve years. She was in the ICU for 74 days, as one infection after another ravaged her body.

Our whole family was together for Christmas, but Karis didn't know it. At the end of December, Karis finally began emerging from her second thirty-day coma. Dave wrote, "Karis woke this morning long enough to open her eyes and smile at Debbie before going back to sleep. **One Karis smile on the eve of the New Year: the renewal of hope**."

In early January when Rachel had to return to Wheaton College, she was comforted by knowing Karis would soon be taken off the ventilator. Karis was released from the ICU January 17. We were told she was the most severely ill patient ever to leave that ICU alive. Dave wrote:

> Karis is out of the ICU! Alleluia! Deb and Karis read Psalm 126. Seventy-four days in ICU or seventy years in Babylon are about the same, don't you think? Debbie is so full of joy she's ready to dance in the hospital corridors. Celebrate with us! You deserve to celebrate after all you've been through with us! Shout it in the streets! Why not?!

Psalm 126
When the Lord brought back his exiles to Jerusalem, it was like a dream!
We were filled with laughter, and we sang for joy.
The other nations said, "What amazing things the Lord has done for them."
Yes, the Lord has done amazing things for us! What joy!
Restore our fortunes, Lord, as streams renew the desert.
Those who plant in tears will harvest with shouts of joy. . . .

Next goal: rehab!

Karis with Dan while recuperating from her second transplant:
hair and hope regrowing

CHAPTER 14

Stripped

Ages Twenty-One and Twenty-Two
Jan 2005-Jan 2006
Pittsburgh, São Paulo, Pittsburgh

Still being "alive" was a dubitable privilege when Karis emerged from coma in early January 2005. She was so weak she couldn't lift a finger to press the call button. She had no movement in her right leg and foot, and no expectation that she would ever walk again. Despite our prayers, she had suffered such intense nightmares while in coma that when the sedation was lifted she woke up terrified, afraid of everyone but me. She couldn't figure out what was real or not real. If I left her side when she was awake, or wasn't there when she woke up, she panicked.

Karis believed the nurses were trying to poison her; she shrank and turned away from dear friends and family members when they came to visit. She was tortured by nightmarish scenes that she endured over and over in her dreams: watching family and friends being murdered by other family members and friends; suffering sexual and every other possible form of abuse; hanging suspended from a helicopter as it swung over Pittsburgh. . . .

The scope of Karis's mental and emotional suffering was unimaginable. For months, she had to ask me whether this or that cousin or friend was still alive; whether this or that one had ever been prosecuted for what they had done. While our consuming concern for two and a half months had been whether Karis would survive even the next hour, Karis "knew" within her nightmares that she would not die. This was part of her distress: death was not an available option of escape from the horrors she was suffering.

Karis was frustrated that we had been so worried for her. Why hadn't we *known* she could not die? Why had we posted so much on her blog and so "exposed" her to the world? Having suffered abuse in her coma nightmares, she felt unbearably vulnerable.

Apparently there was a slimmer line separating Karis's coma-world from our world than the doctors led us to believe. Helicopters, for example, figured heavily in Karis's coma-world. In the ICU, we could hear helicopters landing and taking off from the roof of the hospital. Interestingly, so could she. During the long weeks of her coma we had all taken turns reading to her the *Chronicles of Narnia*. When she woke up, she noticed the set by her bed and said, in the whisper-voice that was all she could manage for months, "Oh, I am so *sick* of those books!" When asked, she denied awareness that we had read them to her, but in some part of her brain she did know! She also claimed to be tired of her favorite music CDs, which we had played for her continuously through the weeks of her coma.

We had saved Karis's Christmas gifts for her to open once she woke up. For days, she was so upset about having missed Thanksgiving, Christmas, and New Year's she refused even to look at the packages. Her family had spent endless hours at her side, but Karis felt cheated. Her father and siblings were gone now, back to their own lives, and she had missed out on the precious holiday time together.

Karis wasn't able to feel grateful for anything. She felt angry, but could express her feelings no louder than a whisper during the weeks it took her throat to heal from her long intubation. She had lost her graft, and the muscles of her body were so atrophied she could do nothing for herself. She had hoped this January to return to Notre Dame for spring semester. Instead, she faced weeks of hard work to regain the ability to move her fingers, her arms, turn over, sit up. . .

Karis couldn't move her right foot and calf. Her foot just flopped. We were told that this type of neuropathy could be caused by extremely high blood sugar, serious infection, high fever, and high doses of certain medicines. She had experienced all of these. She had an enormous, painful bedsore on her tailbone, deep enough to expose the bone. Healing took months.

Having NO INTESTINE meant Karis had two several-foot-long plastic drainage tubes attached to large collection bags, one coming from her stomach and one from the small piece of native duodenum[13] still left in her body. She would have to drag these drainage tubes around with her until she was strong enough for another transplant. If she sometimes felt

---

[13] The duodenum is a short section of the small bowel that connects the stomach, pancreas, liver, and gall bladder to the jejunum, where much of digestion takes place using enzymes from all of those organs.

"ugly" before, imagine now. Our friend Cole mercifully designed and sewed cloth "sheathes" to put over the tubes, to hide the gastric contents that flowed through them.

Karis could not eat or swallow anything, a fact her stomach did not understand. Sometimes she was so desperately hungry she would put something in her mouth, chew it, and then spit it out. If she accidentally swallowed, her drainage tube clogged, causing nausea and vomiting until the tube was cleared. As she struggled through one day at a time, we (thankfully) had no idea she would have to tolerate all of this for A. Whole. Year.

Frankly, my memories of 2005 are a blur. Perhaps I've blocked out some of the pain. Without Karis's blog and other clues to what happened, I would not be able to reconstruct very much of it. I was in full survival mode, eased from time to time by the generosity of sisters and friends who allowed me some breaks from the relentless regimen of Karis-care.

Following her one weekend at home after her transplant, Karis was in the hospital seven and a half months straight, facing one complication after another. We saw God work miracles, and we fought along with Karis for restoration of baseline health, snarled by the development of chronic pancreatitis, an extremely painful condition which she could not tolerate without narcotics. Karis said, "My life is like riding a roller coaster in the dark: I can't see the next curve coming."

The transplant surgeons told us they had made a mistake in transplanting only an intestine the first time, because the innervation of Karis's stomach was no better than in the rest of her digestive tract. When she was transplanted again, if she reached a point of being strong enough to re-list, it would have to be multivisceral (multi-organ), including her pancreas. At that time the number of people in the world who had undergone an intestinal transplant followed by a multivisceral transplant could be counted on one hand.

One day in March, two months since Karis had been released from the ICU, she and I gathered our courage and had a bold conversation with

Dr. M. We started by asking whether he could give Karis a pass to attend Easter services. He agreed, if she was stable on that day.

Karis then asked whether he would consider letting her go to Notre Dame in May for her former classmates' "senior week" before their graduation. Dr. M's eyes widened. He asked several questions, set some conditions, and said we could work toward that idea.

Karis and I looked at each other, took a deep breath, and said, "Can we ask one more thing?"

Dr. M started laughing. "I see your strategy—you start with something simple to get me into the mode of saying yes, and go on to more and more risky. All right, let's hear it."

Karis asked to go home to Brazil for a month. With faith and hope, we scheduled this audacious trip for May 18-June 17.

> **Mar 28, 2005** *For Holy Week they held various celebrations at Ascension. One of them was the stripping of the nave.* **My own stripping is perhaps over.** *I've lost my foot and my hair and dozens of friendships, my ability to dance and to sing and to eat and to yell. Even my face is a different shape and I no longer read. So have **I** changed, in essence and purpose?*

> **Apr 30, 2005** *Our family has been through agony together. I watch us emerge so softened to each other, so dear, so pure . . . and I silently wish for us to be together in Brazil this next Christmas. It will be, if it happens, sweeter than any time as a family has been in years. My whole being strains now for home. If I don't make it back I will have lost Brazil more concretely than the loss of Brazilian residency can express.*

> *Dare I praise You for the mystery and misery of this last year? Somehow, yes, somehow I will stand up under it. I worship You, Master. 1 Cor 1:8 "He will keep you strong until the end. He will keep you strong until the end. He will keep you . . . "*

Karis copied this verse in her journal over and over. It was her anchor during these tough weeks.

Friends ate cake for Karis on her twenty-second birthday, but she received the sad news that day of her dog Buddy's tragic demise. Buddy escaped from home one too many times and was run over by a motorcycle. And there was more grief to come.

May 8, 2005 *Papa, I was checking emails . . . there was one from Anthony titled "Happy Birthday" and when I read it I found out he's dating. Since February and nobody told me. I can't complain; he waited an entire year. But a storm of utterly disconsolate tears overtook me when I read it. I'm still crying. I don't particularly want to be alive right now.*

Papa, I'm drowning! Why, why, why have you chosen to destroy me? When I think of Anthony it's the most ridiculous thing on earth for us to be together again, not only because he loves another girl and not me, but because he has continued to <u>live</u> and **I have become nothing***.*

Nothing. I sleep. I wake to nothing. To alone. I lean on Mama as if she were my arms and legs—she even reminds me to breathe. People—strangers—write from far away and claim they care about me. But Papa, what have I done to deserve that? Do I even care about them?

Tell me the Promifé[14] promises are mine. *<u>All</u>. Lord, any part of my heart that isn't yours—any part that still holds to a love that was over more than a year ago—take it. I hate this. I don't want to cling to it any more. Take this, my death, and give me a new life. I ask this in complete desperation.*

In May, Karis was deemed strong enough to re-list for transplant of pancreas, stomach, duodenum and intestine. On May 10 she was released from the hospital, and we drove to Notre Dame for Karis to join her

---

[14] Promifé was the missions trip on which Karis received the promise and the prophecy (described in chapter 6).

former classmates in their senior week before graduation. A new brace for her damaged right leg and foot was ready the day we traveled! It fit her perfectly and gave her greater mobility during her time at ND. When we arrived on campus, forty friends welcomed her in a joyful reunion.

Both the Notre Dame trip and the Brazil trip immediately after it were huge challenges for me. ND was a dry run for figuring out what Karis needed to get through a week. Multiply everything by four to accommodate four weeks in Brazil, where we would not have easy access to replacements.

At Notre Dame, we had to juggle Karis's medical routine with her classmates' activities. Some things, by then, she could do for herself, but many she couldn't. And who wants Mom around during college senior week? It was a bittersweet experience—the delight of seeing her friends again combined with the vulnerability of being seen as she had become, drainage tubes, near-baldness, awkward gait and all, including by Anthony.

Karis was gracious and kind when she met Anthony's girlfriend, but later she sobbed her heart out. The return to campus accentuated for her so much that she had lost since leaving a year before. She was alive, yes. But what just-turned-twenty-two-year-old wants to live or be seen in constant pain, unable to walk normally or eat at all, toting huge drainage tubes protruding from her tummy, on a demanding schedule of IV infusions and other therapies?

Previously at Notre Dame, Karis had been a star, both academically and socially. But she had emerged from her long coma initially unable to read more than a sentence or two, unable to spell even simple words, unable to do simple math. Tutoring in these basics was part of her rehab program. The drugs had messed with her mind and the road back was tortuous and humiliating.

We returned to Pittsburgh on May 16, with just one day of turnaround before leaving for Brazil!

> **May 16, 2005** *I was already cuddled in bed—but I began to be alive again, so I had to get up and record this moment. It happened so subtly,*

but suddenly I realized that for the last few minutes I had been creating poetry, and hoping and planning about tomorrow . . . I think this all started, or is rooted, in yesterday morning.

Yesterday at Cornerstone [Karis's church in South Bend], *as we sang about laying our crowns at Jesus' feet, my mind filled with my friends— their amazing accomplishments, the honors earned, their plans and dreams for the future. And there I was among them with nothing to say or give. I was among the flowers, but I had been ground by the mower and destroyed even as they bloomed. And then the words came softly to me to replace the word "nothing."* **I too had a crown to lay down**. *It was a crown of thorns, a crown of suffering, of being* **stripped**. *Stripped of my feet, my intestine, my love, my friends, my mind, my dog, my joy. I had no happy news except for the miracle of my presence, except for the fact that I was alive and there, however uncomfortable, awkward, broken. So with tears streaming down my face, I laid down my crown.*

I could write a book about our adventures traveling to Brazil, all of our luggage allowance taken up with Karis's medical paraphernalia. But what a joyous homecoming! She was welcomed by her dad, Rachel, twenty, home for the summer, and Valerie, seventeen, completing her junior year at PACA. Dan, almost twenty-four, joined us for a few days later on.

Karis's friend Gustavo was her chief companion during our month in Brazil.

May 22, 2005 *Gustavo has not feared my pain, but rather taken it upon himself. He knows what pain is and what poetry and prayer and faithfulness are.*

Reflecting on this time years later, Gustavo wrote:

In 2005 when Karis came to Brazil, without her first transplanted organ, we went out to walk a bit. I said: 'Karis, I do not know how far you can walk; please tell me when we should go back.' Well, anyone who knows Karis a little knows she only mentioned the idea of returning when the pain was unbearable to the point of not being able to take another step. Her dad had to pick us up and when we were home, she had to take IV Dilaudid. Karis was never irresponsible; simply, for someone who was given no hope by the doctors ever since she has known herself, to risk everything she had was what it meant to live.

Karis had a check-up with her beloved Dr. G. The next day we left for the beach, one of Karis's deep desires. We capped off her drainage tubes so she could spend a few minutes in her swimsuit before nausea overwhelmed her.

In a blog post June 2, Rachel described Karis as she was at that time:

I last saw Karis the day she got off the ventilator (January 11 or so). Compared to then, she's another person! Her walking is improving and she's gradually getting off some of her meds.

Yet I somehow expected with her coming back to Brazil that she would completely be her old self. It hasn't been that way. Last time she was here, she lit up any room she walked into with her personal shine and vitality. Presently she doesn't have energy to go out much and is exhausted after doing so or after friends come to visit.

She spends a lot of her time on the couch in the living room. Going anywhere, even in the house, takes concerted effort. Her memory, reading, and writing are not back to where they were before the comas, and she knows it. Her voice is still hoarse. We believe these things will improve with time, but it is hard to maintain that perspective.

I only recently understood the situation with Karis's legs. While her left leg is getting stronger every day, her right leg below the knee continues to have no muscle to it. She walks by using her upper leg muscles to lift and move her lower leg. Whenever she goes out she wears a brace.

What hits hardest is her inability to dance. I have never seen joy, freedom, and grace quite like Karis's when she dances. My prayer is,

"Lord, let her dance." Will he do so? I can feel his smile as I think of her dancing in the past, and I know her joy and freedom in those moments were reflections of His glory. No matter what happens, God is working out beautiful and sacred plans for her life. He loves her more than we ever could.

Jun 5, 2005 [translated from Portuguese] *People's emails are a complete contrast with the direction of my thoughts. While I am thinking, if I were a dog they would already have sacrificed me, the emails are full of glory. People who hardly know me but read my story through the blog send me letters full of hope and profound joy at all that God is doing and planning for my life.*

On June 17 Karis and I said our teary good-byes and began our travel back to Pittsburgh. Her dear Notre Dame friend Vera was there to meet us. Karis and Vera had planned to live together at ND while Vera completed her fifth year of architecture school. When that became impossible, Vera managed to find an architecture internship in Pittsburgh and spent the rest of the summer living with us!

The depression Karis had been fighting took on new dimensions when she no longer had her Notre Dame and Brazil trips to look forward to. In August, we were told her liver was damaged irreversibly from complete reliance on TPN. Karis was now listed for transplant of five organs, and her liver deteriorated rapidly. Friends called her "golden girl" as jaundice became pronounced.

August 25 marked one year since Karis's transplant. In that year she spent 249 days in the hospital, 92 of those in the ICU. I wrote on her blog,

> But what we like to focus on is God's incredible grace to us through all the ups and downs of the last year. We have seen God's love and kindness dramatically revealed through the Body of Christ. He has supplied our financial needs in unbelievable ways. We are very grateful.

What happens next? We don't know, and I'm glad I don't know. The ONLY way to walk this journey is one day—sometimes, one hour or one minute—at a time, in absolute dependence on God's daily-renewed mercies. That hasn't changed, just because we know better than we did a year ago what scary kinds of things can happen post-transplant.

Karis's "job" was to grow stronger in preparation for her second transplant, but there came a tipping point when liver failure swamped her. December 1 we were told Karis's MELD score[15] was now 40 (out of 40). Her jaundice deepened to dark orange, her hair brittle and green. Without transplant, she would not survive many more days or weeks. Our family did all we could to fill Karis's life with good things, including a lovely Christmas with all of our family together—though not in Brazil, as Karis had hoped.

Dec 17, 2005 *Having dedicated these last couple of years almost entirely to my own care, I have become what I loathed and feared: bored, self-centered, essentially out of touch with both myself and God. In this twilit life of question marks and constant frustrations, it's so much easier just to let Mom dress me than to insist on the pain and discomfort of doing it myself. Overcoming inertia is so difficult.*

But I felt alive walking down the ice-encrusted sidewalk of the Strip today [an international market area] *with Rachel, music booming from the sushi bar, thinking of gifts for my family. There was jubilation in that moment—Your angels somehow reminding me that it's still worth being alive.*

Other moments of joy: greeting Dad and Val as they disembarked from the 28X bus from the airport. Watching Mom emerge from her room to find dinner prepared and the table set. All of them playing on the Dance-Dance Revolution pads tonight. And showing off our "new"

---

[15] MELD is Measure of End-stage Liver Disease.

1997 Plymouth minivan ("Mini" taking the place of Martha's 1987 "Maxi," which has become an organ donor).

Karis wrote her last 2005 journal entry in shaky handwriting, with many words scratched out and rewritten, evidence of how rapidly she was declining.

> **Dec 30, 2005** *Val suddenly and spontaneously laughed out loud when Dad used the phrase "throwing out the baby with the bathwater." It was such a joy, that shocked second when I realized how much of America she has not encountered yet. 18 days until the 18th when she'll be 18. An adult. Able to drive legally* [in Brazil]. *And just a semester away from packing off to college. She showed me her essay yesterday before sending it to the ND application committee.* [One more sentence is messy and illegible.]

January 7, Karis was hospitalized with high fever and pain. There, at 11 pm on January 9, she received a call for transplant! We danced in celebration without knowing yet whether it was a "go." Karis was thrilled when the doctors determined that her infection was under control and transplant should proceed. Dave wrote on Karis's blog January 10, "At 12:15 p.m. Karis went into the OR all smiles."

Two little boys climbed into Karis's lap as she sat in her wheelchair at an outdoor market in Salvador, Bahia, Brazil.

CHAPTER 15

His Body Bears My Scars

Ages Twenty-Two to Twenty-Five
January 2006–May 2008
Children's Hospital of Pittsburgh, Notre Dame, Northeast Brazil

Karis not only survived her second, five-organ transplant—including fifty days in ICU with complications—but over the next seven months became strong enough to return to Notre Dame in August for her junior year. She joined Valerie, an incoming ND freshman. I stayed with Karis in South Bend doing everything for her but go to classes and do her school work, while Karis gradually reconquered her academic skills and her energy. Unaccountably Karis was able to make straight A's, spend a summer in Wisconsin immersing herself in Arabic studies, and in May, 2008, graduate from Notre Dame!

Back on campus, Karis was flooded with memories of Anthony. She missed him terribly. He, meanwhile, was taking steps toward becoming a Franciscan friar.

> **Oct 13, 2006** *Tom asked me whether I trusted You. I burst into tears. I asked what needs were. If needs are "what we need to survive," yes, I trust You. But other needs? Have You consistently met any one of them in the past? Then why should I trust You in that way? I trust You to be good. I trust You to accomplish Your purposes, but I don't pretend to know what those are.*
>
> *Master, in saying this, I don't mean to ignore any of the multitude of great things You have done for me. What I have trouble believing is that You love me. That anyone but my own family could ever actually love me. Except of course for a few souls for whom the love of ugly things has become a way of life. I don't know quite how to say what I mean.*
>
> *I do know it's easy for me to imagine You disowning me. Do I believe Your love is fundamentally like Anthony's? Is that the deciding factor rather than the transplants and the physical difficulties? I do know that had Anthony been continuously supplied with love for me, I would be in a completely different place, emotionally and spiritually, from where I am today.*
>
> *Kutsal* [sacred one, in Turkish], *I get my very name for You from his language. I let go of him because I knew You had said "**seu amado está guardado**." My dependence was on You, not on him.*

123

But, Master, You know more than I how much I gave my heart to him. He was forever cautioning me to guard it. I guess that is part of why I can't blame him for what he did.

Lord, I stubbornly believe You read my notebooks. That before a word is here You know it completely. But You have attacked me like a bear. If I can't blame Anthony for loving me and then ceasing to; if I can't blame others for their human limitations; if I can't blame the transplant surgeons for all that has been taken from me; then You are left—the Presence beside me, not only in me but outside of me and entirely Other, whom I have to face and the most impossible of all things: allow to love me. It sounds incongruent, impossible to me now. To be called Yours. To stand under a shower of grace. The maxim "life isn't fair" isn't going to cut it this time. I need more than that.

In May 2007, Karis and Anthony re-encountered each other at Wheaton College, each there to celebrate a sister's graduation. Karis wrote, after a long, healing conversation with Anthony soon afterward back at Notre Dame, "*So many glorious and exhausting unexpecteds today in my talk with Anthony. Afterwards I was able to sleep, sweet, a rest unequal to any I have had in the last three years—no, longer—since Jan 2004. Release.*"

Several years later, Anthony also commented on this freeing conversation with Karis:

> One of the biggest ways I experienced Karis's love was in how she forgave me. I hurt her a lot, breaking our relationship. I carried my guilt around with me, refusing to be completely open about it with her. I knew that my honesty-without-love had hurt her and I was trying to not make the same mistake again. When we finally opened up about this, her forgiveness was immediate and complete and left me feeling free of the guilt.

For most of her last two years at Notre Dame, Karis struggled with the painful and debilitating impact of avascular necrosis in her hips,[16] a side

---

[16] Avascular necrosis is death to tissues in the joints caused by decreased blood flow.

effect of longtime steroid use. She was no longer able to bear weight, and had to move to a handicap-accessible apartment which could accommodate her wheelchair. One day Karis threw herself from her wheelchair onto the grass beside Saint Mary's Lake, wailing her distress and despair. Jesus came to her in a vision. On *his* broken body were all of *her* scars.

I wept when I read Karis's description of this precious, profoundly healing vision of our Lord. She wrote:

> **Sep 23, 2007** *My bones are decaying. And with them, I fear, my spirit. Teach me to love, Master.* **May they say this of me when they say nothing else, when I am gone: she loved me. God loved me through her.**
>
> *Thank You, Father, for the vision You granted me of* **the woman breaking her perfume over Your feet.** *Teach me to accept the brokenness of my clay jar that used to contain so much joy and articulation and grace. Teach me to offer it up anew each morning.*
>
> *And* **for this new vision—You with arms outstretched to hug me to Yourself, my wounds on your body** *. . . I will treasure it always. May it grow in me until I begin to really understand Your love for me. For the world. Your fellowship in our sufferings and the grace of our fellowship in Yours.*

Academically, Karis focused on Arabic and on everything to do with sub-Saharan Africa. She wanted to become an informed, compassionate, and articulate voice for women and children there.

> **Oct 6, 2007** *My hands are full of the* **gift of the Arabic language.** *It eclipses all my other interests. Professor R said I had a gift. . . . There is significance in this that cannot be denied.*

Karis developed close friendships with several guys during this second period at ND, especially in the graduate school where the students were closer to her own age. One in particular she dated for a while. But only

Anthony did she ever believe to be her Amado. No one else so resonated with her heart.

To our delight, Karis was able to come home to Brazil for Christmas of 2007. We made a plan to fulfill the high school senior family trips neither Karis nor Valerie had been able to enjoy. For Dan, we had gone to Manaus, to the great Amazon. For Rachel, we had tasted the intrigue of the Pantanal, which left a permanent imprint on Karis's soul. Val chose the Northeast as Karis had desired: the cities of historic Salvador, and Natal with its bright white dunes and crystalline waves.

We caught the red-eye flight from São Paulo to Salvador on Christmas Day, and stayed with two dear single sisters who organized a huge dinner party Christmas night with all their relatives. After touring Salvador, including the old slave market now transformed into a huge city market selling just about anything a person could think of, we traveled north to Natal, to a beach house nestled into white sand.

Dec 25, 2007 Salvador da Bahia [Translated from Portuguese] *This is the first Christmas I've experienced in the Land of the Sun, Bahia: sucking on mangoes, seeing giant turtles, getting to know historic Salvador. The cultural shock was great, but what lovely people: hospitable and warm. It took me time to get over feeling awkward, deformed, and ugly in the presence of their graceful loveliness. It wasn't their fault; it was my own inner tormentors; my usual struggle with how to relate to a group of new people who don't (or maybe do) know my story. I was weary, and a little suffocated by the attention and care of my family and by the necessity of exceptions made for me at every turn.*

Jan 3, 2008 Natal *We are such a complicated family. I revel in this microcosm of complexities. I have only nine days left when we return to Sampa [São Paulo]; so many people to see and things to do. Master, this is what I miss that I used to enjoy here: gracefulness. Graceful shape, curve, gesture; moving smoothly in and out of groups, through worlds. But if I need these scars in order to emerge into full, broken, frustrated humanity, so be it. Put Your ring in my nose and Your lamp to my path.*

Jan 2008 São Paulo *The most important part of myself is hidden here, in the pages of my journals.* **I begin to feel revived, at times almost myself.** *. . . You envelop me with a peace that is new. Permission to let go. Not to be driven. To allow my body to be less strong; to leave an interesting book unopened; to admit things I know nothing about without mentally adding them to my to do list or my "if only" list. Just let them go. To sense hunger and not move immediately to stop it. To know I am sick or sad, and just let it be. These are all steps in the right direction, looking myself in the face and taking stock of what is there— and what is not.* **Beginning to learn wellness.**

Jan 13, 2008 *Sunday. On the plane with Val, gently settling into the idea of being back at ND, buying books and cleaning house and buckling down to conquer my incompletes; seeing everyone again.*

Lord of our many-faceted lives, thank You for these patient days at home, for the rest, for the margin. For the faithful, inexhaustible love of my family. **Returning to Brazil reminds me that my life is a miracle, engineered minutely by God and men. And if my survival is a miracle, then too my coming path.** *I need not fear inadequacy. I will work hard this semester, always seeking Your guidance.*

We didn't know that this special family vacation would be Karis's last visit to her beloved Brazil.

Back at Notre Dame, Karis's insurance mandated that she leave the security of her Children's Hospital doctors and move to the adult intestinal transplant program at Pittsburgh's Montefiore Hospital under Dr. K. It was a challenging transition to start over with a whole team of doctors who didn't know her.

January 24, 2008 Karis was told that her hip could fracture at any time; there was no solution now except hip replacement. This matched the increased pain she felt, which affected sleep and her ability to focus. But Karis was determined to finish the semester. Her orthopedic care was transferred to Pittsburgh in preparation for surgery after she graduated from Notre Dame in May.

May 5, Karis's friends threw a huge party to celebrate her twenty-fifth birthday. Before the party, Karis received an urgent call from Dr. K, telling her she must drop everything and travel to Pittsburgh immediately—she had a blood clot in the celiac artery which supplied her liver and intestine.[17] Karis simply said no. Life-threatening or not, she refused to give up the joy of celebrating her hard-won victory at Notre Dame by attending her commencement ceremonies.

Dr. K was so concerned that he or someone in his office called back multiple times, and finally he called me. I pledged to drive Karis directly to Pittsburgh after her graduation (later amended to "after her *party* after her graduation ceremony").

Proud friends and family gathered from several countries the weekend of May 16 to honor Karis for her achievement. Invited to offer the invocation at the Honors Assembly, she drove her blue scooter right onto the platform and offered a prayer that even strangers commented on as being the highlight of their weekend. Possibly no one was more grateful than Karis for reaching this milestone.

> *Father God, holy Crafter of the universe, As we come forth to receive our honors from men, may we recognize that all the honor and glory belong to You, and be freed from false modesty to rejoice in what You have accomplished through our dedication, perspicacity and hard work. Come, Lord, and rejoice with us today at this our celebration. . . .*
>
> *We worship You for the way You have fashioned us, pounding all the leaven out of us, throwing us on the wheel, raising us up as receptacles under Your deft fingers. Fill us, today, now and always, that Your presence and peace would accompany us to the four corners of the Earth,*

---

[17] Wikipedia justifies Dr. K's concern: "The celiac artery is an essential source of blood, since the interconnections with the other major arteries of the gut are not sufficient to sustain adequate perfusion. Thus it cannot be safely ligated in a living person, and obstruction of the celiac artery will lead to necrosis [death] of the structures it supplies."

and bring us home. Make us unafraid, even of being crushed and recast, because of our trust in Your hands. . .

Karis's resident years at Notre Dame ended, but the university's impact on her never would. Her deep affection, gratitude, and loyalty were immeasurable. Our family was not saying good-bye to ND—Valerie had two more years there—but we would not again have the same close relationship with the faculty, staff, and friends there who had encouraged, supported, and believed in the possibility of Karis's success. May God reward them.

"Once a Domer, always a Domer."[18]

---

[18] ND students are called Domers, a reference to the golden dome on the administration building.

Karis graduated from Notre Dame May 18,
2008, riding her blue scooter.

CHAPTER 16

Crushed

Age Twenty-Five
May-December 2008
Pittsburgh and Tahlequah

"We were crushed and overwhelmed beyond our ability to endure.
But we stopped relying on ourselves and learned to rely only on God.
Now he uses us to spread the knowledge of Christ everywhere,
like a sweet perfume."
2 Corinthians 1:8b-9; 2:14b

After Karis's graduation party, we drove through the night from South
Bend to Pittsburgh. Dave and Val drove the moving van with Karis's
furniture, piano, etc., and I following with Karis stretched out on the back
seat of the car. We arrived at Montefiore in time for a 6:30 a.m. blood draw
and transplant clinic.

Dr. K decided that surgery to deal with the clot in Karis's celiac artery
would be too risky, but he had no confidence that medication alone would
be effective. Her hip replacement would have to wait until the blood clot
was resolved. Since nothing dire had happened in the two weeks since Dr.
K had called ordering her to drop everything and run to Pittsburgh, Karis
apparently was not inclined to take his words very seriously.

May 19, 2008 *Yesterday I graduated, and drove through the full-moon
drowse of hail, into the crickets and bird-chirp outside 5030 Centre
Avenue Apartments in Pittsburgh.*

*This morning I heard again those weary words, "danger" and "fatal."
I look past them blinking the dryness out of my contacts; look past
them to the immediate: Mama's oatmeal cookies, coffee and cream, a
crossword puzzle and sweet thoughts of my friends, voicing aloud my
thanksgiving for all the generosity that has gone before and behind me.
I'm choosing with Mama how to arrange the furniture in our new
home-for-the-summer.*

*My vision once again narrows, so quickly, so deftly, and I am back in
Pittsburgh as if the Notre Dame glory were a fold in the blanket. I am
a child again. One of many to be handled, to be taken care of: best-
case-scenarioed and mistaken about.*

Dr. K said both "your life is quite possibly over" and "what we all have to do right now is calm down and not ask questions." He said this to my perfectly calm, undemanding exterior. He said it to Mom—or maybe to himself—looking into my eyes. My self is already frozen; there is no purpose in urging absolute inertia to stillness. If I just go on ignoring Dr. K, will my body go away?

Karis, Valerie, and I lived in a small apartment for the summer while we waited for Karis to be stable enough for surgery. Dave joined us for part of July. Rachel and Dan returned to Brazil and DC. Val prepared for a year away in Bologna, Italy, to strengthen her Italian major. Karis, in unremitting hip pain, used her journal to sort out her hopes, frustrations, and faith. Again, she reviewed the promise and the prophecy that were so significant to her.

> **May 2008** *Soon I will be able to walk, and dance; this is my hope.* **I have Your promises to stand on. Meu amado está guardado. My life is to be somehow a door to the nations; a key will be given me.**

> *So I will survive the hip replacement surgery. Or at the very least, You will use this short life I have lived. That seems huge enough comfort not to fear taking the next step: I shall not fear evil. Nothing bad can happen to me. Though I die, I die to You as I have lived to You.*

> **Jun 2008** *If You need my pain, Lord, it's Yours. You can have it!*

> **Jun 2008** *On the way back from clinic we passed a gaggle of kids and their mothers under hijab chattering away in Arabic. Had I not felt so physically wiped, I would have joined them. Perhaps next time, if there is a next time.*

Karis formed a wonderful friendship with a family from Libya who lived in our apartment building. As I write this, nine years later, I have just enjoyed a Facebook exchange with them!

> **Jun 2008** *When has a plan of mine ever worked out? I laugh at my plans in order not to cry. I have no argument for why You ought to*

pave the way. I have no will even to stand up for myself. But I know You hear my prayer. Father, please, I want to go to Percy's wedding in Minnesota [Anthony's younger brother, in Valerie's class at ND, who had become a dear friend].

Jun 14, 2008 *I woke early (a little after 5) and with oxycodone in my system read for a long time, comparing the Bible's Old Testament accounts with the Qur'an, my mind hungry for comprehension.*

Jun 15, 2008 Shadyside Hospital *Thank You that my hip surgery is still a go tomorrow. I choose this moment to remember with simple thanksgiving.*

Jun 16, 2008 *The surgery is off. I have four urinary tract infections, and my liver numbers are high. Is it worth wondering when the surgery will be? Or how much more pain I can tolerate?*

But looking to the next intention, I am reserving a hotel in St. Paul for Percy's wedding! Then the nurse comes in and wow—her boyfriend is Brazilian; she's looking to learn Portuguese! Every other person I meet is fascinating or fascinated; mostly both. So how can I complain? Maybe this was the only way for You to arrange the Minnesota trip. Certainly Your hand is still on me.

Karis's hip replacement surgery was rescheduled for July 2. She would have to endure several more weeks of unrelenting pain. But she had Percy's wedding to anticipate, traveling to Minnesota with Valerie!

Karis knew of course that Anthony would attend his brother's wedding. Still, seeing him again was an emotional shock. Anthony believed God was calling him into the Catholic priesthood.

Jun 30, 2008 St. Paul, MN *"Yes, baby, I'm alive." I whispered it into Valerie's hair. I am so thin now, so fragile. I have survived but as yet not much more. I still love Anthony, wrenchingly. I have not become the person I wanted to be. I have finally been able to sob. I worship You, Lord, with my tears, with the oxymoron of my feelings right now:*

*the anger, the submission, the joy, the full love. I feel the scarred body beneath my tunic even as **I see Your own arms wide for me, scarred as I am.***

*Master, in agony I question You, with eyes wide open and arms, too. Did You mean all this to happen, Anthony for the priesthood and me for the—for whatever this is? Master, Lord, Kutsal, Reb: I somehow had this pipedream that You would care for me, for my soul, no matter what; that **I was hidden in You and "nothing bad could happen."** Do You remember that evening when despite the pain and having been held back from the prayer vigil at PIBJI, I realized it and danced for joy in You?*

But now, Father, I cannot dance. It is not the collapsed hip that keeps me from it. It is the crumpled soul, the self-hatred, the alienation from my body and the—dare I say it—denial I have lived in.

Denial of what? Of the fact that it seems, Father, You have abandoned us. I don't mean just me, although my own tears could fill buckets (call them self-pity if You want—I need to cry them so You might step into them). I mean my Beloveds. Master, I need to call You to account for them, as well as for me. Lord, have mercy. Lord, please take care of me.

Papa, I have come now to listen to You. I have uttered my needs and You have heard them. I have expressed them with full hope, Potter, that You will meet them.

Why did You tie my heart so fully and irrationally to Anthony's? Why, if this fracturing was the destiny; this wedding perhaps the last contact I will ever have with him?

> *Even after the amputation*
> *like a ghost-limb*
> *my love remains:*
> *his name accidentally*
> *on my tongue in every casual conversation.*
> *And though my eyes, my will*

tell me the pain is only in the air—
tell me there's no arm there—
    fingertips keep reaching for the flute.[19]

Master, while we're at it, what is in Your mind regarding me? Because if You don't have some great purpose in this, if You are not indeed forming me in ways that are invisible and mysterious to me, and caring for me in ways my heart has not seen—I want to curse Your face. If I am to be lost, in the shadows, cast off and forgotten and unused, why live? Why not take Job's wife's advice?

*My only, my Beloved, my inheritance: give me the will to live. **I would kiss Your feet and cover them with my tears and wipe them with my hair** if only You would speak to me. If only I could believe we were on our way somewhere, the two of us: me and the Trinity.*

God did speak to Karis. But what she understood him to say dismayed her: she was to pray for Anthony and for his family every day for the rest of her life. She challenged God on how he could expect her to "get over" Anthony, while at the same time having to think of him to pray for him daily. Yet her conviction was strong that this was exactly what God was asking of her.

After much struggle, she agreed to try to do this for one year.

Jul 2008 *Master, sustain this fragile soul. I am full-dependent on You to remind me and teach me **how to keep the promise I made today: to pray for Percy and Anthony and all their family every day this year.** Speak, Lord. Let me taste Your love.*

I knew nothing about this commitment, nor the fact that Karis initiated e-mail communication with Anthony so she would know how to pray for him. Years later, Anthony told me he had no idea Karis was still in love

---

[19] Anthony is skilled on the flute.

with him, nor the promise she had made to God to pray for him daily, nor what this cost her. He imagined she wrote similar light-hearted emails to other friends, casually asking how she could pray for them. It seemed consistent with Karis's habit of praying for everyone she knew.

Karis came through her July 2 hip replacement surgery well, though she was unprepared for how difficult the ensuing four months of physical therapy would prove to be. Soon other problems appeared. Her life was a yoyo between home and Montefiore Hospital with infections, bowel obstructions, and dehydration.

Valerie, Rachel, Dan, and I flew to Guatemala August 9-20 to celebrate the dedication of my dad's translation of the New Testament into Maya-Ixil, his life's work. Karis was not stable enough to travel with us, a huge disappointment. All my siblings, most of their spouses, and seventeen of Dad's twenty-five grandchildren joined him for this very special event, enjoying the unique beauty of Guatemala and many stories of our growing up there. Meanwhile, Dave's sister Kathy stayed in Pittsburgh with Karis.

My father was not well our last days with him. We assumed it was something he ate or drank, plus fatigue from the exciting events of the dedication and family reunion. Later, back in Tahlequah, he assured us he was fine.

After seeing Val off to Italy upon our return from Guatemala, I prepared to move. We had sub-let just for the summer, thinking Karis would then be well enough to pursue her own plans and I would return to Brazil. But until her health stabilized, I had to find another place for Karis and me to live.

Battle and Carol's third-floor apartment, where we had lived for two and a half years prior to Karis's return to ND, was rented to other people, but they generously offered Karis and me their guest room for an open-ended time. The guest room was within Battle and Carol's own living space, not an ideal arrangement for them. And it was difficult for me because I had so enjoyed having our own space, a sense of home within the daily rounds of medications and treatments, transplant clinics and hospital stays. But we had run out of money and had to depend on the kind hospitality of these dear friends.

What should we do with an apartment full of Karis's furniture, kitchen equipment, etc.? She gave it all to a family moving to Pittsburgh, transferring it from our apartment to theirs the day we moved out.

At the end of August, on the heels of a bowel obstruction, Dr. K shocked us by declaring it was time to find out why Karis was having so many intestinal issues. He scheduled exploratory surgery for just a few days later, September 3! This surgery lasted thirteen long hours. When Dr. K finally emerged at 11 p.m. to talk to us, he explained that Karis's insides were a huge mess, with intestines wrapped around and through her liver and other organs. Everything was so stuck together it was difficult even to distinguish what was what. No wonder she had been having such severe intestinal problems over the last months!

In trying to separate Karis's intestine from other organs, the surgeons had to sacrifice her ovaries, so Karis was thrown into instant menopause. And rather than creating a new ostomy, Dr. K made the decision to connect her intestine to her rectum. We were shocked. This "experiment" had not gone well when Karis was a child, and we had no reason to expect this time would be different.

At first, Karis embraced Dr. K's assurances that soon—once her body had the chance to adjust—her intestine would function without an ostomy. He was sure we would soon be grateful for what he had done. But her recuperation from this surgery was very rocky, including complete lack of control of her intestinal output. Added to this was Karis's grief that she would never bear the daughter she had dreamed of. For two weeks, we did not see her smile.

September 28, twenty-five days post-surgery, Karis was discharged from the hospital, but a week later was readmitted with a bowel obstruction, frantic with pain. In the ensuing days she lost twelve pounds. Her skin, no longer protected by an ostomy, was burned and ulcerated by her intestinal output, rich in caustic digestive enzymes.

I was so tired after days and nights with Karis in the hospital that when I had the chance to go home for a while, I sometimes didn't remember where I had parked the car. At times I threw myself on Battle and Carol's guest bed and crashed into sleep fully dressed.

Dave came from Brazil to stay with Karis while I traveled with a brother and sister to Oklahoma October10-17. We helped Dad move from his house to assisted living. Mom, by then, was in a "lockdown" Alzheimer's/medical unit. Shocked to see Dad with jaundiced skin and eyes—clear signs of significant liver dysfunction—I insisted he see a doctor. October 20 (his eighty-fourth birthday), while my sister Jan was with him, Dad was diagnosed with cancer of the gall bladder, too far metastasized to treat.

October 23, Dr. K agreed to let Karis travel to Oklahoma to see her Granddad. We joined some of my siblings there October 26, a precious time. But Karis began to have increased pain, bloody stools, and fever. November 2 my sister Karen, who had young children at home, flew with Karis back to Pittsburgh, taking her straight from the airport to the hospital. Karis was not in rejection as we had feared, but was suffering from infected ulceration of her rectum.

Dave flew from Brazil to Pittsburgh so I could stay with Dad in Tahlequah. Unable to eat, Karis continued losing weight. She had no open veins for insertion of a central line for TPN. She hoped to return to Tahlequah to say a proper good-bye to her granddad, but the infection spread into her transplanted bowel, causing severe pain, fever, and ongoing bloody diarrhea.

Dad died November 12. His eight children sat around his bed for hours imagining him enjoying his many hobbies and interests in Heaven. The loss for us was enormous. Dad was taken from us too soon.

The day Dad died, I was informed that Karis was now in severe rejection. Dave scheduled a flight to join us for Dad's memorial service on Friday, November 14, cancelled it because Karis was in such difficult straits, then upon her insistence, rescheduled. Dave and I hadn't seen each other for two months, and I tried to tell him I wasn't coping well with all the stress.

During my father's memorial service, though, we received a call that Dave's dad had just died! Dave flew to Florida while I returned to Karis in Pittsburgh.

Attempts to insert a central line continued unsuccessful, severely limiting Karis's options for nutrition and treatment. Soon her veins were so "used" no one could draw blood even for basic tests. Finally, with people around the world praying, a doctor managed to insert a mid-line PICC[20] in Karis's right arm through which she could receive IV medications. The PICC, though, was inadequate for TPN, so her weight loss continued.

November 18, I recorded on Karis's blog a promise we were holding on to: "Your strength will equal your days" (Deut 33:25). Karis's EBV[21] was now over a million (normal being zero). The docs had to stop treatment of rejection in order to fight the EBV. While she was so vulnerable, only immediate family were allowed to visit.

Dan joined Dave and Rachel for PopPop's memorial service in Florida November 19. Dave and Rachel flew to Pittsburgh the next day. The Browns' guest room could not accommodate all of us. Generous friends offered us space—three bedrooms!—in their home for two months. We moved there November 22.

November 24, Karis's precious PICC became dislodged from her right arm. After persistent effort, another midline PICC was placed in her left arm, but there was still no apparent access for a central line for TPN. On Thanksgiving, she was allowed to suck a Popsicle.

"Miracle of miracles," as Dave said, Karis came home from the hospital December 2, after one month of intense treatments. The doctors wanted her home because her immune system had been destroyed in treating the

---

[20] PICC stands for "Peripherally Inserted Central Catheter."

[21] Epstein Barr Virus (EBV) causes mono (mononucleosis), which compromises the liver. For transplant patients, with their immune systems suppressed to protect their grafts from rejection, EBV is life-threatening.

rejection, making her extremely vulnerable to infection. But our delight in having Karis "home" (in our new home-away-from-home-away-from-home) was short-lived. During December, she was in and out of the hospital four more times with a chain of complex problems. Her liver began showing signs of stress; her skin and eyes took on a familiar but unwelcome yellow cast.

One December day Karis had just been discharged from the hospital when her intestine once again began bleeding profusely. We had to turn around and take her back to Montefiore, and something broke inside of Dave. He suddenly recognized that Karis was not going to get better, and that he therefore had to move from Brazil to Pittsburgh. Since his commitments were scheduled a year out, working out this decision was challenging, and for all the ensuing months he battled discouragement and depression.

Friends Débora and Brian traveled over Christmas and offered us the use of their home, allowing both us and our host family to have our own space for a few days. Valerie came from Italy and Dan from DC. With Rachel they made the space festive, even putting up a Christmas tree! We spent Christmas Eve with Karis in the hospital, and she was given a pass to join us at the house for a few hours on Christmas Day.

December 27, I wrote on Karis's blog, "Liver distress usually causes lack of energy, and that certainly is Karis's case. She wants to stay awake, but her body just wants to sleep. Every so often I catch her smiling, and she tells me she's remembering how special Christmas was."

Despite everything, God gave our family Christmas joy.

A healing Christmas, December 2009
Valerie, Karis, Debbie, Rachel

CHAPTER 17

Broken

Ages Twenty-Five and Twenty-Six
January-December 2009
Pittsburgh

The events of the second half of 2008 left me exhausted, bruised, and confused. I entered 2009 hanging on by an emotional thread. It seemed that my wellbeing didn't matter to anyone. I felt like my husband went into depression because he didn't want to have to live with me and share the burdens I carried. From my jaded point of view, Dave chose to go into his own self-centered little tailspin over leaving Brazil and *having* to give support to his wife and family.

Clearly, we were both overwhelmed. It's easier, of course, when we take turns being stressed out, so the other one can more effectively offer support. 2009 didn't provide us that luxury. At some point, Dave told me he was hurt by my lack of empathy in his huge crisis. I, who felt invisible to him through that whole year, simply had no words. The gulf between us in that moment felt un-crossable. I told Dave I would prefer he stay in Brazil than come to Pittsburgh as one more person I had to care for. Our marriage hit perhaps its lowest point in our history.

Reflecting on this tough time, Dave wrote:

> Broken. Karis broken physically and emotionally. Debbie broken in deep burnout. Me broken in depression, realizing I had to leave Brazil, my calling, my team, my ministry, my life.
>
> For both Deb and me, our own struggle felt greater than the other's. Neither of us had emotional margin for helping with each other's agony, paralysis, loss of energy, and hopelessness.
>
> In 2009 Karis reached the brink of death four times. Each time God intervened, but it would take Debbie and me many years to fully heal individually and as a couple from the stresses that swamped us.
>
> In tangible and measurable ways, though, God freed me from my depression. A major piece of my healing was getting help from others. God gave me Allen, a new friend who reached out and became my closest ally in Pittsburgh. My team in Brazil, seeing my hopelessness, listened to my heart and ministered God's heart to me. My son Dan was very present for Debbie and Karis and for me as well, firmly but

lovingly confronting me with my need to move to Pittsburgh. These people carried me much like the four men who carried the paralytic to Jesus.

I've learned that the 2009 disconnect between Dave and me is not unusual. Divorce rates in families with chronic illness are cited between 75 and 90 percent. Normal tensions in marriage are amplified many times over by the needs of a child who requires special care. In our case, we lived in survival mode not just for days, weeks, or months, but for years, with few breaks, and most of the time living apart.

Karis's unpredictable roller coaster left me feeling powerless before the physical suffering she had to endure and the many losses she was hit with one after another. Even with all the support we had, financial pressures were enormous and negotiating payments was draining and time-consuming.

Once again, I felt displaced, as if I had no personal identity other than as Karis's mom. I didn't know how to achieve a place of our own, that our whole family could consider "home." In various ways we were concerned for our other three children. Both Dave and I had lost a parent. There seemed to be no opportunity for me to mourn my own loss of our beloved Brazil.

The consequences of not adequately addressing my burnout became very costly to me and to dear ones around me. I attribute the survival of our marriage to both God's grace and Dave's stubbornness. He believed in our marriage against all odds.

Where exactly was God in this picture? In 2009, God seemed as distant as my husband. I couldn't find him. He hadn't changed, so the fault must lie in me. While in a sense that may be true, I twisted it into unhelpful self-judgment. I began to blame myself for my husband's apparent lack of concern for me.

The enemy of our souls knows our vulnerabilities and has no qualms about exploiting them. My logic went something like this: God never gives us more than we can handle. I feel overwhelmed; therefore, I am handling things inadequately. Anyone else would be able to deal with my circumstances with grace, courage, unflagging faith, and endlessly sacrificial love. I am a wimp.

This logic did not motivate me to reach out for help, from God or from people. I put more pressure on myself to do better, to carry more, and to "complain" less. I acutely felt the debt I owed to anyone who came to my own or Karis's aid in any way. Rather than taking me toward and into community, my desperate needs isolated me. The enemy of my soul had a heyday.

2009 started off very rough for Karis, her weight down eighteen pounds (from her baseline of 105 pounds) from no TPN and unstoppable diarrhea, three-four gallons a day ulcerating her skin. Dr. K finally recognized the need to restore her ostomy, but he felt she had to get stronger to tolerate the surgery. How could that happen without a central line for hydration and nutrition?

Three days after this discussion with Dr. K, God answered our prayers regarding a central line! In an innovative two-hour surgery, a catheter was inserted through Karis's back into her inferior vena cava and into her heart. They called it a trans-lumbar central line. TPN was started immediately. And they finally got a peripheral IV into Karis's leg for fluids, medications, and electrolytes. A glimmer of hope!

January 11 was the three-year anniversary of Karis's five-organ transplant. We remembered and named multiple blessings Karis had experienced in those three years, and through it all, the Presence and faithfulness of God expressed to us through kind and generous people. Though I personally felt I was drowning, the prayers of the amazing Body of Christ around the world kept our family afloat.

Karis was still Karis, reaching out to the people around her in the hospital, loving and praying for patients and their families, hospital staff, and visitors. She was especially attuned to the needs of international patients, who had to deal with the challenges of severe illness through the fog of a language and culture they barely understood. Whenever she felt well enough, she could be found somewhere on the transplant unit sitting by someone else's bed, listening to their story and concerns in any one of her five languages—English, Portuguese, Spanish, French, and Arabic—but most often Arabic. Dr. K, an Egyptian, attracted transplant patients from across the Arabic-speaking world.

January 16, Karis suffered the heartbreaking loss—through nursing error—of her costly trans-lumbar central line. Another was successfully inserted in a three-hour surgery; Dr. K called it "the most precious asset in this hospital."

Narcotics given for this surgery sent Karis's mind into a tailspin. I wrote on her blog:

> The last clearly intelligible thing Karis said was, "Why aren't I getting better?" Why, indeed. If we can take a step back, it's actually rather entertaining. Yesterday she pushed the nurse call button several times. Her concerns were to help people get in out of the cold, to get away from the bears, to get more dogs in here, and to take care of the Germans.

> Karis doesn't believe that her sisters aren't in Pittsburgh. She wants Rachel to read to her, not me. She wants Valerie to sing to her, not me. She insists I take her home to Brazil. She is quite sure I could help the nurses get people in out of the cold, if only I would.

On January 18 (Valerie's birthday), Karis suffered three seizures, a new and frightening experience for us and for the Notre Dame friends who were visiting. An MRI showed inflammation throughout her brain, and bleeding in two places. The culprit was judged to be a high Prograf [immunosuppressant] level. January 21, I wrote:

> I'm sitting by Karis in the ICU while she receives a unit of blood and checks e-mail on her little computer. I'm not kidding! That's how much better she is! She just said to me, "I'm so spoiled, being in the hospital." I said, "There are people who wouldn't completely understand that." She replied, "I mean, being so well cared for."

145

Earlier, she had said, "I'm so spoiled" when the nurse gave her ice chips, and again when she was told they're going to start physical therapy.

Karis is mostly making sense now. I asked her what she remembers from last week. She says she dreamed someone tried to kill her, and she fought back. Then Dr. B [her doctor in South Bend] came and rescued her. Her conclusion from this and other dreams is that she wants to live. She had been discouraged enough the last few weeks to be unsure about that. Truly, we *are* spoiled—and grateful.

February 2, Dave returned to Brazil, after almost three months away from his work there. Karis urged him to go, saying in her journal, *"When Dad is in Brazil I feel part of what's happening there, and I really miss that strong connection when he's not."*

February 5, Dr. K decided he *had* to go ahead with surgery to restore Karis's ostomy before anything else went wrong. He reserved the OR for a generous four hours. Instead, the surgery took eight and a half hours. Karis's graft was in bad shape, ulcerated especially in the middle section inaccessible by endoscopy either from above or below. The surgeons inserted a tube to continue monitoring this area post-surgery.

Feb 16, 2009 *Jen gave me a gorgeous* [artificial] *rose, a single tall stem, which Mama hung on the wall in front of my bed. It makes me smile every time I look at it. It looks real, taped as it is upright against the gray-green wall, elegance incarnate. I think I'll give it to Jacira when I'm done here, if she's still alive. If I'm still alive.* [Sadly, Karis's Muslim friend did not survive this hospital time.]

One day Dr. C told Karis she could have one-quarter cup of any liquid. She chose hot tea. We turned the occasion into a tea party, inviting other transplant friends and their families. One of the docs came by to be sure Karis was only *sipping* her tea, not *drinking* it!

Since her surgery September 3—almost six months—Karis had been *out* of the hospital only thirty-seven days and since December 15, only one (part of Christmas Day). No wonder Karis wrote, *"I no longer feel optimism. I am running on empty."*

Feb 27, 2009 *Lord, teach me not to fear. Life is just so unpredictable and it seems everything that could go wrong in my body does. Teach me to love **my enemy, my body**. Help me to grieve, and to move on, and eventually to build again. Help me to become the person You envision.*

March 2, the docs surprised us by releasing Karis from the hospital! March 6 I wrote:

Karis feels better than she has in so long. She didn't take pain medicine the entire day! The first time in weeks if not months. It is wonderful to see her animated, making plans with friends, involved with LIFE! Weight today 94 pounds (she took a big drink before weighing and wore her heaviest shoes—wants very much to see that number going up!).

Monday, March 9, after one lovely week at home, Dr. K surprised us again: he pulled Karis's J-tube and her trans-lumbar catheter! The catheter had a blood clot at the end that could cause problems if it broke free. Sadly, that very evening she went into such copious diarrhea she had to be hospitalized in the ICU, with a blood pressure of 60/40 and heart rate of 175.

I wasn't allowed to see Karis until noon the next day. Dr. C greeted me with, "She's a very sick girl and we don't know why. Without a central line, there's little we can do for her."

After hours of work, they were able to get a central line in by going through Karis's liver, a creative approach called trans-hepatic. With this line, she stabilized. She was delighted that it went in through the front, so she could rest much more comfortably.

March 11, Dan encouraged us with a visit. At the very moment he typed on the blog, "Karis is lucid and able to speak clearly when awake, but frustrated to be back in the hospital, and still in a significant amount of pain," we received a call saying Karis was in rejection. March 15, her

Prograf level went too high, as it had in January. Again she said funny things. On her blog, I quoted one conversation:

> Me: You've been pretty sleepy.
> Karis: Yeah, but mostly just rude.
> Me: Rude?
> Karis (with great intensity): Yes. It's to show those people that President Bush is the victim of rudeness. I have to be rude to them to show them what it feels like. No matter what, this rudeness is completely over the top. It has to stop.
> Me: Let "those people" beware!

The next day, Karis took a dramatic turn for the worse, bleeding profusely from her intestine. It seemed Karis's healing might take place in Heaven rather than in Montefiore Hospital. Dave and Rachel flew in from Brazil, Val from Italy, Dan from DC. ICU nurses allowed us all to gather around Karis's bed.

Once again, though, Karis survived the immediate life-threatening crisis. The doctors told us her only option was to go through *another* transplant. I wrote:

> Transplanting an isolated small bowel into a multivisceral transplant (leaving the other organs in place) has been done once in the history of the world, for a young man last August. He is doing well. So out of a sample of one, we have a 100% success rate!

To everyone's surprise, Karis gradually started getting better! March 30 she was stable enough to leave the ICU. Dan and Rachel, reassured, had left by then, and April 5 Valerie returned to her studies in Italy. April 13 Dave returned to Brazil. On April 14 a Popsicle traveled all the way through Karis's system—the first intestinal transit since this episode of rejection began. Earlier that day, Karis wrote a very shaky entry in her journal.

Apr 14, 2009 *3:51 a.m. I hear a single steady beep from the hallway and feel a certain cahoots with the universe I haven't felt in a very long time. Finally it seems life can begin again in earnest. Mama and*

I are back to the bare bones of usness, with no crazy stunts or seizures or surprises on the horizon. Just getting stronger, more and more well.

I'm not sure how legible this will be. My pen's encounter with the paper is merely an infinitely lesser sign of my soul's encounter with my mind, which has been so long in coming back.

Apr 16, 2009 *Lord, it's not Your absence that baffles me, so much as Your unrelenting Presence. Last night amidst the covers the Holy Spirit came so sweetly, so gently . . . and allowed me to dream again. I thought about seminary, about restructuring the refugee center, about Arabic classes and becoming a part of Ascension's intercession team. Physical therapy. Spending time with Aunt Linda over harvest. I am beginning to wake up again. Emotionally. Mentally. Oh yes. You have carried me gently. You have been here, Your Spirit ever-present, ever-patient, velando* [watching over me].

Shhh, don't tell the nurses! Karis and I made an illicit escape from the hospital. They thought we went to the hospital's little garden. Emboldened by success, we made similar forays into the "real world" with some frequency, and only got in trouble a couple of times . . .

Apr 17, 2009 *Yesterday was by far the best day I've had in months. The NG tube was pulled* [Karis always hated NG tubes!], *and Mama and I and the IV pole and wheelchair went down Forbes Avenue to Rita's Ice. It was full-blown Spring, complete with hyacinths and tulips and Frisbees. The lady at the Chinese booth gave us free Dim Sum. We had good, hard, real conversations, with room for tears. I had a real physical therapy session, sour Skittles and doublemint gum, a bath, Szymborska's poetry, e-mails from Anthony and AL, and Dr. C's triumphant visit telling me my intestine is unaccountably better.*

On our outing, I kept exclaiming over the lovely spring flowers, wanting to tour nearby gardens. Karis, though, insisted on walking down Forbes Avenue in the middle of Pitt campus. She gazed entranced at students' faces as they hurried by. *"Mama, do you think they know how beautiful they are?"*

Apr 18, 2009 *Thank You for the apparent miracle at work in my body. Yes, miracle. What else can I call it? Thank You for my friends and the pain medicine that allowed me to enjoy their shenanigans. Thank You for tea, hot and cold. For soy milk and lemon drops and jelly bellies.*

Lord, help me rediscover myself intact, somewhere. Help me still be capable, or become so again; and recover not just capacity but also content: memories, self, motivation, personality. I am so much less able to truly laugh. I beg of You, make this temporary! Thank You, Jehovah-Rapha, God who heals. I worship You by waiting and eating and sleeping and walking. By sobbing, purging my soul, laying it before You. And I see Your hand, so gentle always. In the middle of the night I wake and see it.

Apr 22, 2009 *Oh, happy day! I can eat again! My biopsies were "some better"!*

It's funny—I just came across several photo IDs—my Library of Congress card, my Notre Dame IDs and my driver's permit. Looking at the photos, I see looking back at me a perfectly viable human being . . .

Apr 24, 2009 *Sometimes you have to bathe the morning in tears until it turns sweet. This morning was like that. Yesterday Dr. A and I decided together to discontinue the Dilaudid and increase the Fentanyl patch. What an incredible relief! I feel clean again. I feel myself again! The pain does take a lot of energy and cramp my ability to do things, but it's better than the psychological torture of trying to evaluate at every moment whether or not it's bad enough to legitimately ask for pain meds and to worry always about dependency. I don't have to do it on my own: they've taken it away. Bless them.*

Not every day was so positive.

Apr 26, 2009 *Today I was so angry, Lord. So angry because my mind was one big fuzzball despite the lack of narcotics. I couldn't wade through the swamp to have a good conversation or read or play guitar or write—to do anything, really. I couldn't even lie there with my eyes* *closed and think coherent thoughts. Why does this happen, Lord? Why does my mind come and go? Why are my emotions so wacky that even I am utterly surprised when I burst into tears? How does Mama put up with it? What possible purpose does a day like today serve?*

Apr 28, 2009 *Thank You, Father, for allowing these tears. I need them to midwife my acceptance of my body, freshly destroyed as it is. The lovely little girl I once was has been banished for good. In its place is a being that will need much love. Much work. May I someday walk with grace again. May I dance. Thank You that even Jesus cried. "During the days of Jesus' life on earth, he offered up prayers and petitions with loud cries and tears . . ." Hebrews 5:7.*

Apr 29, 2009 *Lord, I'm so irritable I could burst. I'm rude and lazy and irresponsible.*

Yet God graciously gave Karis moments of worship and wonder in the midst of her struggles.

May 2, 2009 *Yesterday was speechless. Ecstasy by the window; trembling, drinking in the beauty of the sky. I am alive, and it is marvelous in my sight. Dancing while standing still. Worship. How can I express this, even remotely? The thrill, the awareness of You so visceral. I want to share this. That which You whisper in the dark to me I want to declare on the rooftops.*

*I want to learn about this Earth and her many peoples and their histories and geographies—the different smells of her many airs . . . I want to learn to see her more and more through Your eyes. To hear her groans and to be for them the **fragrance of hope**.*

And special visitors brought encouragement and joy.

May 3, 2009 *Yesterday Paula and Gerry came over. Gerry played his cello. They brought morning glories and violets from his garden and chocolate truffles and an Elizabeth Goudge novel—but most of all they brought their company. I just basked.*

So, Father—instructions for the day?

On May 5, we were informed that Karis's biopsies looked terrible: not a welcome twenty-sixth birthday gift.

> **May 6, 2009** *Yesterday was my worst birthday ever, hands down. Even worse than 2005, when Buddy was run over and I found out Anthony was dating and my class graduated without me and I couldn't eat anything and nobody came by my hospital room to eat my birthday cake because it was Ascension Day at church. Even worse than that.*
>
> *This incorrigible body has one day's hope left to it—maybe that will be enough.*
>
> **May 11, 2009** *I rise today through a mighty strength, the invocation of the Trinity . . .* [she quotes more of St. Patrick's Lorica].
>
> **Thursday May 14, 2009** *Monday I got out of the hospital. Glory. Pure glory. Overwhelming, the smells, the sights, the tastes. The sound of birds. I'm gorging myself on green.*
>
> *My clothes don't fit me anymore. My pants simply dropped off of me as I clumsily mounted the stairs to our second floor bedroom at the Browns' house. I need a belt.*

After another series of crises and hospitalizations, I woke up one morning with a clear conviction: It was time for Karis and me to move. It took us two more months to find a place that could work for us and to figure out that we could use retirement money to pay our rent. But what a happy day it was, when Karis and I moved to our own apartment August 15, and had the joy of returning Battle and Carol's home to them. Having our own home, our own space, gave both of us renewed energy.

Meanwhile, unknown to me, all this time Karis had continued praying for Anthony.

Jul 31, 2009 *I pray for Anthony, that You would give him joy and boldness, and light in his eyes—but not the light of combat. I pray for his near-murderer and for the family of the German businessman who died in his place.* [Anthony had been threatened in Istanbul.]

Anthony's voice echoes in my life, from my love of hummus to the way I describe to the nurse the reason for my stomach being so loud. It's the oracle, I say—it only speaks Turkish.

Karis reflected on her experience of the last few years.

It becomes easy to forget the 18-year-old who left Brazil with so much less scope and less fear. But she's holding on to the same arm that is under hers even now. And He's still guiding. **He's taken her and broken her over His feet—she's spilled out, broken, destroyed**—*all her being feels twisted beyond recognition. Her body cut up and sucked out and bloated, but not just her body. Her eyes are smaller now; her voice too soft and slightly childish. She stutters, often forgets the end of an intended thought or entire sections of her life. Looks dully at her best friends while they bring their joys—engagements, children—and can't express gladness though she tries. Limps at best, falls over or flings herself with no balance from one place to the next. Is already somewhat deaf* [fallout from her long periods on the ventilator]. *Is awkward around children, always needing special treatment—the soft chair, the lactose-free custard, the clean bottle, someone to help her carry her share.*

This is not who I wanted to be. I never imagined I would stay in these comfortable United States, that I would or could consume so much; be the "delicate" one. But I'm not complaining, Lord. You know I'm not. I just want to know **where to spill the perfume**.

The central story of the last months of 2009 is a pneumonia which almost took Karis to Heaven, and almost broke my marriage. God brought Karis back once more. The trauma, though, had far-reaching consequences, confirming that Dave must move to Pittsburgh. Dan had reached his limit of having to be the "man of the family" in Dave's absences, sacrificing his own life to be present for Karis and for me whenever crisis hit us. Dan still cared as much as always, but he no longer jumped in his car to start driving to Pittsburgh every time it seemed Karis's life was threatened.

Several years later, in 2015, I suffered from post-traumatic stress disorder. Some of my nightmares and 3-D flashbacks related to events surrounding this pneumonia of September 2009. I offer the following story as a glimpse into the marvelous ways God can intervene and heal our deepest pain.

One afternoon in 2015, I related to Dave and to our counselor, Ginger, an intrusive memory that had been plaguing me:

> Walking into the ICU one day I heard men yelling at each other. Through the doorway to Karis's room I saw the director of the ICU on one side of her bed and Dr. C on the other. The ICU director shouted over Karis's inert body, "But if we do that, she will die!"
>
> Dr. C shouted back, "If we *don't* do that, she will die!"
>
> My knees buckled. It was all I could do to hobble back to the waiting room, where I sat shaking uncontrollably, overcome by panic and despair.

As Dave and Ginger prayed for me, Jesus walked into the waiting room and sat beside me. I shrank to the size of a two-year-old and he took me in his strong arms, cuddling me close to his heart as I wept.

When my tears calmed, Jesus asked whether I would like him to go with me to see Karis. I reached up to grasp his fingers as we walked back into the ICU. Apart from the hums and beeps of the machines, Karis's room was quiet now. Jesus pulled up a chair and anchored me again on his lap while he cradled Karis's bruised and swollen hand and began to sing to her, sometimes in English, and sometimes in Portuguese. I rested against him and let the music fill me, soaking healing into my tattered soul.

How long were we there? I don't know. It was a moment outside of time. I learned later that as Jesus sang healing into me, the person who had the next appointment with Ginger called her to cancel. Dave and Ginger sat there with me for the whole next hour. When one of them gently told me it was time to go, Jesus walked with me back to the waiting room, and as we walked, I gradually grew to be again a middle-aged woman, capable now of facing whatever would come next.

This healing time with Jesus was one of many precious experiences of grace in 2015, gradually freeing me from years of trauma. I am so deeply grateful.

Even in the midst of all the distress of 2008 and 2009, God unaccountably gave me the energy to complete a reflection on my experience with Karis that I called "Worshiping God in the Desert," which was published in Brazil in 2009.[22] No doubt this work also helped keep me afloat, as I traced God's faithfulness to us through our wilderness pilgrimage.

Could we have survived 2009 without the far-reaching network of prayer fueled by Karis's blog? I don't think so. Our friend Ted and then my brother Steve managed her blog for a long time. Even in the ICU as he prepared for open-heart surgery (a six-way bypass!), Steve faithfully passed the oversight of Karis's blog to his daughter Becky, who set us up with a Wordpress format we could manage ourselves. For all of this, too, I am so deeply grateful.

My sister-in-law, Elaine, commented to me, "Both of these—the blog and *Worshiping God in the Desert*—encouraged our faith as we saw God's faithfulness to you, and your response of faith as a family." This is one more example of the mystery of God's power seen through the cracks in our fragile jars of clay (2 Cor. 4:7-10).

2009 concluded with a gentle time together which eased some of the strains our family ties had suffered. As Rachel, then Valerie, then Dan arrived for Christmas, Karis's world at least temporarily righted itself. I didn't know until later that Dave had finally laid his love for Brazil on the altar. All I knew was that he was different somehow, more attentive to me and to our children. A breath of hope stirred between us.

---

[22] *Karis, A história de uma mãe e a luta de sua filha,* São Paulo: Editora Mundo Cristão, 2009.

Karis was HOME for her twenty-seventh birthday!
She hated her "chipmunk cheeks," a side effect of long term steroids.
For a long time Karis refused to let me post
photos of her on her prayer blog,
because she didn't want to "gross out" her friends.
In her neck is the miracle central line that lasted the rest of her life.

CHAPTER 18

Where to Spill the Perfume

Ages Twenty-Six and Twenty-Seven
January-December 2010
Maine, Pittsburgh

Stronger in 2010, Karis invested ever more love in her Arabic-speaking friends. She made use of multiple hospitalizations and clinic waiting times to listen, weep, laugh, and pray for these dear ones, spilling out to them the fragrance of Christ. My part was trying to keep her intact and well enough to have energy to give to others, and help her keep track of her commitments to them.

The first major event of 2010 was Notre Dame friends Chrissy and Ben's January 2 wedding in Maine. Karis and I and the transplant team had been working toward this trip for weeks. We were very excited to board the plane on Wednesday, December 30, with Karis's bridesmaid dress, gifts, and all her medical paraphernalia. A bowel obstruction in the midst of a blizzard, though, resulted in her missing the wedding and having to be life-flighted back to the ICU at Montefiore, the gift of Chrissy's bridal bouquet in her hand.

Karis was taken once more for attempted insertion of a central line. This time, a new doctor in Interventional Radiology managed to get a catheter through the internal jugular in Karis's neck by forcing it through scar tissue.[23] What a miracle—what a gift! Dr. K said, "I'm going to take that young man out to lunch!"

An IJ, as this type of line is called, is usually used only temporarily, and only in the hospital. Karis used this placement for *four years*. Each time a catheter got infected or clotted, skilled doctors were able to insert a new one in the same vein over a wire. Thus, God provided a way through our wilderness of no venous access without again having to go through her back or her liver.

Karis was released from the hospital January 13, in time to prepare for her friend Vera's wedding January 31. This time, Karis walked beaming down the aisle, supported on the arm of another bridesmaid.

---

[23] A risky procedure—a few weeks later, trying the same thing on another transplant patient, he ruptured her vein.

Ever the optimist, Karis made plans for becoming more independent and for all she wanted to accomplish in 2010. As usual, though, reality at home trumped the great ideas she had while lying in a hospital bed. For starters, this was the bitterest, snowiest winter in our Pittsburgh experience. Since we parked on the street, this meant extra effort shoveling whenever we went anywhere, and required extra protection of Karis from the cold, which she could not tolerate.

Jan 13, 2010 *I spoke with Mama today about how good it was to have received the total sacrifice of herself at times I needed it but that I need to take my own responsibility for waking up for my 8:00 routine, my meds, my ostomy, and my exercise, and be more careful about library due dates and fines, and getting places on time. Teach me, Lord, to be time conscious and to plan within my bounds . . . I want to prioritize my independence going home. I also want to investigate the Arabic immersion program at Georgetown, and get back to work on Greek and Spanish and Portuguese literature. And shop for and make my own food . . .*

After testing of her limits resulted in a fall on the ice that split open Karis's knee, a friend with cerebral palsy confined to a wheelchair challenged her on when she was going to accept her limitations and stop talking about all her plans for the future.

Feb 19, 2010 Montefiore Hospital *Last time I wrote Jeanine had asked me when I was going to get over my 26-year-denial and realize I was disabled. I felt scalded. I literally bent over and gasped for breath. Disabled? I suppose, when I think about it, I was born missing intestinal nerves as some are born missing their eyesight or a leg or some element in their brain. But my uncle, for example, has a shriveled arm and leg—that hasn't defined him as disabled.*

Jeanine only wants the best for me, and she's been hearing me talk like I'm living for tomorrow for so long, I understand where she's coming from. But that does not mean I should accept it. I do not believe my setbacks to be permanent. Nor do I generalize them to all of life—individual incidents are just that.

Maybe having the memory of a fish is a great asset in resiliency! Often I just sit like a weaned child on Your lap, Lord; a child on Your wide beach. I can do this because there is abundance in You; I can trust You to provide. Because of Mama, basically, I have learned total security; a sense of contentment in all things. I can take enough manna for today, doing few things but doing them well.

As to accepting myself as permanently disabled, I think it would kill me.

May 1, 2010 [Very shaky handwriting after a bowel obstruction] *Dad has been so good at caring for me while Mama is at a church retreat. I plead for each of my transplant friends who are suffering right now: Angie and Pauline and Wijdan and all of them.*

May 6, 2010 HOME *Yesterday was my 27th birthday. It was a great day. Everyone cancelled on Mom and me, so not only was I able to sleep in, stretch, feed the fish, check e-mails, eat breakfast—I got a shower, the first in a week and a half.*

Karis was well enough to travel with Dave and me to South Bend on May 13th to celebrate Valerie's graduation from Notre Dame. Val's boyfriend Cesar was there from Brazil. Karis was delighted to see ND friends and honor her beloved sister. We returned to Pittsburgh with Valerie and all her things on May 18th, anticipating Val's departure with Cesar to Brazil for two months. In her journal, Karis reflected on what she knew of Valerie's Brazilian beau.

May 26, 2010 *This is Cesar's first time in a different country, so I wonder what he is like in his own context. He is thoughtful, hardworking, dedicated, willing to try new foods as long as they're not vegetables. He plans ahead and is disciplined. He loves his family and really loves Valerie.*

God did something very special for our family that summer. Separately,

Rachel in Brazil and Valerie at Notre Dame had told me they wanted to live near Karis for a time. I was delighted—and sad. Our apartment was small; I had no place to receive my other two beloved daughters.

I was weeping over this before the Lord one early morning when I heard banging outside my window. Looking out, I saw our landlord hammering a sign into the yard that said "Apartment for Rent." I rushed out and learned that the flat on the second floor, just above ours, would be available in July! "I'll take it!" I said impulsively.

The arrangement was perfect. Rachel and Valerie had their own space, but to see Karis or join in family dinners or fun, all they had to do was run down the stairs! Rachel lived in that second-floor apartment for four years, first with her sister, then with a roommate, and finally with her husband.

Valerie's intent was to go to nursing school at Pitt so she could work at Children's Hospital, wanting to "give back" in response to all that had been given to Karis and to our family when Karis had been a patient there. Rachel chose to pursue a master's in social work at Pitt, and while a student there, met her special someone, Brian.

There's more to both of these stories, of course, but five years after the girls moved into the apartment on Morningside, in the summer of 2015 we delightedly helped both couples move into houses of their own in Pittsburgh. Dave and I never dreamed we would have our adult children so close to us, with Dan in DC, only four hours away. For Dave and me, this proximity has been pure delight.

> **Jun 4, 2010** *Bless me in my efforts to better communicate in Arabic with those I have come to love (O, F, F, W . . .) and those I will be meeting. May all I say build Your kingdom and not break it down: conversations deep, constructive, and purifying.*

Sadly, in the second half of 2010, despite our best efforts to support and protect her, Karis fell multiple times, always with injuries. This became a discordant, unhappy theme for the rest of her life. She so wanted to function independently that she constantly tested her limits, often with disastrous results.

I will not chronicle all her falls, but it seemed Karis lived always with stitches in various parts of her body, most frequently her legs and knees, which several times required skin grafts. Due to the steroids she took to prevent rejection, these injuries took a long time to heal and often became infected, sometimes resulting in hospitalization. I told everyone, "DON'T say, 'Karis, don't fall'—that seems inevitably to lead to her next tumble!"

Jun 10, 2010 [Written across the page in a variety of calligraphy styles, each word a different color] **Marvel Exult Take joy Be glad Rejoice** *We are so limited in our words! I am well enough to go home—but first the Arts Festival! Thank You for the perpetual summer of the soul.*

Jun 11, 2010 *Yesterday at the Arts Festival we stopped at a booth of clothing made from wax batique. I found myself looking into the wrinkled, laughing face of the vendor and asked him if he was Ibo. He was caught off guard. "How did you know I was Ibo?" I must have blushed. "I don't know. You just . . . look Ibo." I had a lot of Nigerian friends, I told him. And he had mentioned he was from Eastern Nigeria, so the options were Ibo, Yoruba or Hausa. He didn't look at all like Ibrahim (Hausa) or Kunle (Yoruba), so he was Ibo. I'm glad I was right—he got a kick out of it. It was a good time.*

Jun 19, 2010 *Tonight Dad called to say he has rented our São Paulo house to another missionary family. Thank You, God! I have to get to sleep now. It's 3 o'clock in the morning. But first I pray for . . .*

Jun 28, 2010 *I heard a friend retell the story of the alabaster jar, the image that has been so precious to me of **being broken and spilled out over Your body to perfume Your Church: that the waste of my life, my expensive life, might serve the Church once I am gone. And that the memory of me would somehow strengthen the Church to endure whatever persecution or death it is to face.***

The same story has been there for me throughout the years, always gaining more significance. It has been a comfort that God gave me warning and choice in the way He would use my weakness to His purposes. And it has given me a kind of cahoots with God, this intimate participation in His planning. Along with His Pantanal promises and those from Promifé (oops, I've been using third person as if telling You about Yourself!), You have reassured me completely, that I might live in peace.

But the image gained in significance again when You used it to encourage and confirm Your desire that I really invest in intercession ministry.

*You also spoke to me through prayer time with Carol A of Your strength in my weakness; the way You've got my back—and my hands. You used Carol's words, Your own words: **Pour out all of yourself like the woman with the alabaster jar.** Pour out your entire effort and all of your energy as **perfume poured out to You.***

A series of crises took Karis to a special moment of emotional release:

4ᵗʰ of July, 2010 Montefiore Hospital *Lord, just hold me. Scruffy, dirty, tearful me. Snot running down my chin, thumb in mouth. Let me curl up into a ball on Your lap and sob myself to sleep.*

Too much has happened in the last few days. It's just built up in me, the tension. I need to release it and draw near to You again. I love You, Lord. Show me how I can bless those around me, even here.

An example of how God answered this prayer is evident in the following entry.

Jul 15, 2010 *Thank You, Father, for the family I met yesterday in clinic waiting room. Muhammad, the father, so kind. He told me there are two types of people—those you pity and those you admire. He said he could tell that I was one to admire. It was a shameless xaveco [flattery] but it was so good to turn my perspective around and see myself as someone who could potentially be admired. His wife, Zakaria, has had* *the majority of her small bowel removed and is pre-transplant. I'm not sure how much English she speaks. I spoke Arabic well. Thank You, Father, for encouraging me through them.*

We longed for Karis to have an extended time OUT of the hospital so she could have a life again, making progress rather than the "one step forward, two steps back" rhythm she was in. But Karis used her clinic and hospital times to the hilt. Intestinal transplant at Montefiore was like a United Nations, so many were the countries and languages represented. As usual, Karis invested most in the Arabic speakers.

> **Jul 22, 2010** *So many glories. So much heroism here. And I free like a bee among them; small and unthreatening. After clinic I went up to 11 North to visit people there. It was cool to be a visitor instead of a patient, everyone saying how wonderful I look.*

Karis's friend Suzanne recalls:

> I remember Karis's bruised split knee, and how it was simultaneously terrible and beautiful. I wish I had taken a photo or painted it. I told Karis how amazing it looked and she readily agreed. Karis greatly encouraged me with learning Arabic and practicing it with her. I remember being in her hospital room with her saying words and having me point to objects in the room. I still think of that when I hear the word mustashfaa which means hospital but sounds a bit like mustache.

> Over the course of several years, Larissa and I met weekly with Karis to share life and to support each other with prayer. I was always struck by how Karis neglected her own more urgent needs just for the sake of not inconveniencing us, and spent most of her time thinking of others rather than dwelling on her own pain, discomfort and deterioration.

August 18, Valerie arrived from Brazil to begin her nursing studies and moved into the upstairs apartment with Rachel. I wrote the next day in regard to Karis's fall after trying to catch a Frisbee:

Musings on mercy: In Dr. C's gentleness, Patty's zeal for us, and even Nancy's scolding, I see a picture of God's faithfulness to us. We knew Karis's newly split knee was our fault, and that we were in for some deserved rebuke, but we didn't think even for a moment that we should go somewhere else to get it cared for. We weren't afraid the docs might say, "OK, that's it. You went over the top this time. We're not going to waste our energy any longer investing in you."

Just so, when our souls are battered and bruised, we run straight to God for help and healing. Even when we've hurt ourselves by pushing our limits or rebelling against them, we can count on his care. He knows us completely but still accepts and loves us. *"So let us come boldly to the throne of our gracious God. There we will receive his mercy, and we will find grace to help us when we need it most"* (Heb. 2:14-18 and 4:15-16).

Entering this September, 2010, I realized we had much to be thankful for. Her September 2008 and February 2009 surgeries had set off a long series of complications. In September 2009, Karis had almost died from pneumonia. 2010 had been so much better! From September 2008 to August 2009, Karis spent 220 days in the hospital, thirty-eight of those in ICU.

In contrast:

Sep 2009-Aug 2010, only 99 days in the hospital, 31 of those in ICU
Only 11 ICU days since October, 2009 and none since February
One month with NO days in the hospital! November 2009

Since May 1, only 20 hospital days; **best 4-month period in the last two years**

No rejection since June2009 (**15 months rejection-free!**)
Last dependence on TPN, Jan-Aug 2010 (and doing well without it!)
Last time on such a low dose of steroids: probably 2008
Last fall with injury . . . hmm, let's not go there!

September 10, our hearts broke with dear friends Débora and Brian when their beautiful son was stillborn. The day of his funeral, a woman from our church was buried who was four days short of 101 years. Mystery.

In her September journaling, Karis expressed some insights that, all these years later, surprise and touch me. I was well aware of her resistance to her forced dependence on me, but didn't realize how clearly she was able to view this from my side.

> **Sep 15, 2010** *Bless Mama with good sleep and freedom from worry about my kidneys. Mama is overwhelmed and exhausted, burnt out in a profound way. Maybe she is human. Most of the time it doesn't seem so—she denies her own needs and thoughts so often, as a pattern of life that's engrained in her. We're both so insecure about our roles vis-`a-vis each other. Should she treat me as a 27-year-old, or as a child? Sometimes I am one and then another in the same minute.*

> **Sep 24, 2010** *I have been absolutely horrid to my friends and to my mother. Father, the more I think about it, I see how flaky I have become: absent, distant, inconsistent, moody, unreliable. Constantly inconveniencing them because of Not Having Control of my health and my time.*

> *Some things I have no control over because I'm dependent on rides and never know what my blood sugar/pressure/ostomy/hydration status is going to be. But I can work to overcome them. I can resolve to honor people with my time. I can set aside the laptop when Valerie comes back from school. I can react immediately when Mama calls me to dinner. I can keep her apprised of what is going on, especially when I'm mentally depending on her for transportation.*

> *I need to be more articulate, to respond even when I don't have a good, full answer. I need to restore the belief within myself that my word means something; that when I say I'm going to do something I'm accountable for it. I need to create awareness that people are sacrificing other things when they spend time with me. But not to feel guilty—to take the honor and return it.*

> *I have been acting out of a certain sense of debt with most relationships that are dear to me. It's like I'm saying constantly* **"I know you want Karis. I can't give you Karis—I miss her too. Maybe someday by some miracle she'll come back. But until then all you've got is me."**

Rachel commented upon reading this: "Oh, man. We were all feeling this."

> **Later** *After dinner Rae and Val and Mama and I worked on a jigsaw puzzle and had a Real Conversation, the breakthrough all of us had been needing. Thank You, Father, for this precious sharing time. May this day, September 24, not be forgotten. May I learn the value of other people's time. May I continue conversations with Val and Rae and Mom, getting to know their hearts.*

I still didn't know that Karis was communicating with Anthony, keeping her promise to pray for him daily.

> **Oct 2, 2010 Hospital** *Anthony sent me an invitation to his initial Franciscan vows on September 4. He then spent a couple of weeks in Turkey with his family and is currently settling in to the theological institute in Assisi to begin studies in philosophy. Generally, he says, seminary takes around five years.*

> *After dinner Mama and I walked 21 times around the hallway, a whole mile. It's amazing the number of people one ends up interacting with in a day without even turning on the computer or making a phone call or stepping off the unit or even barely leaving bed: M and E, M, M, H, T, L, P, J, Dr. C, A, T.* **Finding ways to spill the fragrance** *You have given me.*

Karis ends this brown journal on October 6, saying, *"Life is full and too good for words."*

Most of Karis's writing in her new journal the last weeks of 2010 is prayers for her friends. She suffered from so much intestinal distress those weeks that on October 18, the docs put her back on TPN. Karis's Saudi Arabian friend Oujdan died that day, after months of struggle. Oujdan's husband kept in touch with Karis by phone for months after he returned home.

For several years, Karis had engaged in a successful fundraising effort for CEVAP, the Compassion ministry in São Paulo she had participated in during high school. She was deeply disappointed that her efforts were not enough to save this transformative ministry to slum children.

> **Dec 8, 2010** *I received a letter from Gisele today about CEVAP. Gisele was chagrined and not sure how to break the news. They have voted to close CEVAP down at the end of the year. I was singed in spirit. Show me, Father, how to respond to Gisele.*

> **Dec 18, 2010** *Dad answered my question about the fear of the Lord, defining it as "caring more about the Lord's opinion than anyone else's, even your own." This is what I want, Father. This is how I want to live, for the chapters of my life You are still writing for me, until You take me Home.*

Through all these months in and out of the hospital, Karis filled her journals with prayers for her friends and loved ones, asking the Lord how she could pour out her life for their sake. Surely, her prayers themselves were an effective spilling from her alabaster jar over the precious Body of Christ.

Our family at the Elliott reunion in July, 2013
Front: Rachel, Valerie, Cesar; Back: Brian, Debbie, Karis, Dave, Dan

CHAPTER 19

Father, Let's DO Something!

Ages Twenty-Seven to Thirty
January 2011-January 2014
Pittsburgh

2011 was a busy year for Karis, in which she continued to pour out all she could in love and prayers for her friends, both inside Montefiore Hospital and out. It was also a year of many losses: the heartbreaking deaths of several transplant friends, and at times, the loss of mental stability due to the many medications Karis had to take as she balanced on the rejection/ infection tightrope.

At the end of May, we moved from the apartment into our own house, thanks to an inheritance from Dave's parents that afforded us a down payment.

> **May 31, 2011** *God invited me at the beginning of this year to trust Him, to **drink in the rain often falling on me** and produce a crop worthy of those for whom I am farmed. He showed me it would be a difficult year but in the end He would accomplish his purposes. Each of our family members was facing enough trauma and transition to consume the family's energies and attention for a very stressful year. The situation seemed impossible.*
>
> *But You, oh Lord, gave me a sniff of the possible and drew me into Your cahoots. Winked. The One enthroned in heaven laughed. So I have such a sense of anticipation and trust and love.*

In the days following this journal entry, Karis dealt with skin grafts on her legs, worsening rejection requiring IV steroids, infection of both knees, infusions at 6:30 a.m. eleven days straight at 7 West (Montefiore's transplant outpatient infusion center), often after little sleep, the death of another transplant friend, and two short hospitalizations.

Snapshot of a "typical" 7 West or Clinic day:

My alarm went off at 4:45 a.m. so I could run a one-hour antibiotic infusion before we had to leave for clinic. Karis could sleep until 5:30, so unless I had to clean off the car and shovel snow, I had time for a shower and to throw in a load of laundry before I had to get her ready to arrive at transplant clinic at 6:30 a.m. The routine for 7 West was similar, but we might be there all day.

Karis was a night owl, whose ideal sleep schedule was 2 a.m. to 10 a.m. She considered getting up at 5:30 a form of abuse, especially as chronic fatigue deepened along with her kidney failure. She had increasing difficulty with making simple decisions, so I had to be more and more firm with her if we were to get out of the house on time: "No, Karis, you may not change your mind about what you're wearing today." "No, Karis, sorry, you're stuck for breakfast with what you chose last night . . . and with what you're taking to do in the waiting room. Sorry, there's not time to wrap another gift for a friend, or to make another list . . ." Karis loved to make lists. It made her feel more in control of her life.

The next challenge was getting her safely out of the house and into the car, especially if there was inclement weather. There was little traffic that early, but the snow plow may not yet have reached our neighborhood. We made the home-to-Montefiore trip so often that we explored every possible variation of ways to get there.

Before transplant was ever an option for Karis, visionary staff and donors at Montefiore Hospital (where Karis's adult intestinal transplant team was based) recognized the value of an outpatient transplant unit: 7 West. 7 West made use of hospital resources so patients would not have to be admitted to the hospital every time they needed an inpatient medication, infusion, or treatment. Despite the inconveniences—especially the early hours—staying OUT of the hospital instead of IN was like gold.

Fortunately, at 7 West Karis could usually have a bed (the other option was a recliner), and sleep away her early wakening. At clinic, we were confined to a waiting room with just one couch where one person could stretch out; everyone else was limited to chairs. I wrote several letters to the hospital administrators complaining about this. Just because they were outpatient didn't mean it was easy for transplant patients to spend several hours sitting up!

Later, as Karis's kidneys failed, she had increasing problems balancing her electrolytes (essential substances like potassium, magnesium, and calcium). This was the principal reason she might have a 7 West day. She might need wound debridement, or a blood transfusion, or a medication that required monitoring for possible adverse side effects. 7 West days were decreed for Karis so often it felt like a miracle if we went a whole week without at least one 7 West day.

Usually we received 7 West orders at clinic. First thing at either place was a blood draw. Patients saw the doctor in the order in which their blood test results came back from the lab. The waiting room hours were a bonding time for transplant patients and their families, time to talk and share, laugh, cry, and sometimes pray together.

Back when she was more mobile and had more mental energy, Karis journaled about a 7 West day:

> **Friday, Feb 5, 2010** *Mom exits the car and comes around to gather our gear and spot me getting out of the car; the valet drives it away. We do this almost every morning coming to 7 West for my infusions. Mama supports me with one arm as we walk through the lobby toward the elevators. Her other arm is laden with too many bags—but honestly, what could we do without? Our two purses, my laptop, food, medications, ostomy supplies, blood pressure cuff and glucometer, my TPN backpack (this one at least on my own back). There is another whole bag of things to do during the hours in 7 West: letters, crochet, books, etc. In this bag are gifts for people we plan to see in the waiting room or visit upstairs* [on the transplant floors; Karis loved gift-giving].

Extrovert Karis thrived on clinic waiting room time, unless she was feeling too sick to handle it. In those cases she was often sent directly to 7 West for treatment, and sometimes ended up admitted to the hospital if the situation was too severe to handle outpatient. With Karis's level of immunosuppression one never knew—she could wake up feeling fine, yet be in ICU on a ventilator by the end of the day. But many times, the services of 7 West allowed her to sleep at home. We are grateful to the competent, compassionate staff who worked with us to make that possible.

My niece Marie came from California to help Rachel and Valerie care for Karis July 20-30, 2011 while Dave and I traveled to Colorado for mission meetings. Karis was "hyper" mentally during this time, not always in touch with the reality the rest of us inhabited. The psychiatrist called it a psychotic break; I thought her steroid dose was too high. She journaled during those troubled days:

> **Jul 13, 2011** *I nibbled at the marrow of a chicken wishbone, carved orchids out of cartilage from spine; I watched the wild turkeys and rings of recent brides and the collarbones of the singers and glimpsed lovebirds in the trees: sea dragons and feather-stars and prime numbers, asymptotes and blood cells and bellies—and tried without trying to remember the color of my Abuelita's eyes. I am swimming in a sea of Your thick waters, buried 'neath the smooth weight of your white floppy creatures, pinned pleasantly by their poundage, breathing spray-cold sharp air from Innisfree.*

While Karis was in her own world, she saw herself in the very presence of God, talking with him about her mental distress. He said to her, "Don't worry. I am tucking your mind within my mind. I am holding it for you." This experience was so vivid that Karis referenced it the rest of her life. Later, when back in touch with our reality, she fretted over whether it "really" happened or whether she had imagined it.

> **Sep 14, 2011** *Teach me, Lord, to fear You. It always comes back to that. Deepen my knowledge of what it is to be a God-fearing woman.*

Karis had another mental breakdown in October. Her last journal entry of the year, October 19, is jumbled and largely illegible. My sister Jan came from Mexico to help us. I wrote:

> This whole thing is complex, as the medication they think will most help Karis can severely impact her liver function, which interferes with other medications, like her immunosuppressant. It has been life-saving for me to have Jan here, as Karis needs much more care than usual; too much for one person. Our trust is in God, who loves us and loves Karis.

In November, Karis was admitted to the hospital with a central line infection, which morphed into one complication after another. She missed the joy of Thanksgiving at our house with a lovely gathering of family and friends, but God did something very special for her that week.

Renée, a friend from Arizona who was in Pittsburgh for Thanksgiving, visited Karis at Montefiore. Karis resisted letting Renée see her as sick as she was. Renée gently asked if she could just pray. She began a "generic" prayer ("Lord, please help Karis to get better . . .") but suddenly stopped and said, "I feel like I'm just babbling. Wait a minute."

Renée bowed her head for a few seconds, then said, "Karis, God wants me to tell you he has tucked your mind within his mind and you can relax, because he is holding it for you." Both Karis and I burst into tears. Renée had spoken the exact words Karis had struggled over since her "vision" the end of July, not knowing whether her encounter with God had been "real" or just her imagination.

Renée had no context for understanding the significance to Karis of what she had just said. I followed her to the elevator trying to explain, but Renée just shook her head, mystified. Karis was able to sleep that night with a peacefulness that had eluded her for months.

After a couple of weeks at home, yet one more line infection set off another series of complications. Karis was in the hospital for 111 days straight, including ICU time and four weeks of in-hospital rehab. Two more transplant friends died during that time. Karis was still deeply grieving for her friends Lacie, Pauline, Angie, Oujdan, and Jamila, so I made the decision not to tell her yet about these two additional losses.

December 16, Karis was granted an hour pass to attend Valerie's graduation from nursing school. Val left for Brazil December 26 to visit her boyfriend before taking a job at Children's Hospital. Soon, though, she called to tell us she had decided to stay in Brazil and find a job there so she could be near Cesar. February 2 they announced their engagement, planning a November 17 wedding in Brazil. Karis now had a huge goal to work toward: a November 2012 trip to Brazil.

Karis couldn't come home from the hospital for Christmas, so we took Christmas to her. Nurses helped us decorate the family lounge and we shared our joy with other patients' families as they wandered in.

By the time Karis came home on March 30, 2012, her therapists told her she was the hardest-working patient the rehab unit had ever seen. She was able to walk on her own using a walker and had re-conquered many of her skills. But this achievement didn't last.

An image that comes to mind is a kaleidoscope: the same pieces of colored glass can be rearranged into an infinite number of patterns, none of which can be secured against a twist of the chamber. Karis worked to achieve a pleasing pattern of the different elements in her life—friends, church, her own studies, her daily disciplines, work on her languages, her self-care and independence—but inevitably, some crisis twisted the kaleidoscope so she lost the pattern and had to start over.

Several factors confounded Karis's efforts to have control over her life. Chronic rejection damaged her intestine and generated so much output that despite IV hydration, she constantly battled dehydration. This hurt her kidneys, which couldn't regulate the fluid in her body, resulting in wet lungs. To be home from the hospital, Karis soon required a new tether, to an oxygen tank.

Karis asked herself daily, through her kidney-failure disorientation and fatigue: How can I be productive? How can I contribute? She hated feeling like a "moocher." *"Oh, Father, please! Heal me or take me Home!" "Father, can't we DO something?"*

And, *"Father, what about Your promises to me?"* Karis was perplexed. It certainly didn't look to her like the promise or the prophecy was being fulfilled.

The one constant, as Karis says frequently in her journal, was the presence of the Lord, **Emmanuel, God with us**. Isaiah 63:9 became a touchstone: *"In all their suffering he also suffered . . . He lifted them up and carried them through all the years."* The only way to keep our balance was total dependence on him, one day, one hour, at a time. Easy? No! Yet how faithfully he carried us!

In May, Karis was well enough to travel to DC to celebrate her brother Dan's graduation from Johns Hopkins' SAIS master's program—her first out-of-state trip since Chrissy's January 2010 wedding in Maine.

Karis's twenty-ninth birthday was shadowed by the death of Maureen Como, the longest-surviving liver-intestine recipient in the world, almost 22 years. Maureen was a "torchbearer" for the rest of us in transplant land, always encouraging those who came into this experience after she did. Her death disoriented us; it was like losing our compass. Every time we lost one of our transplant friends, our world was altered. In these months, there were so many losses it was hard to absorb and grieve them all.

> **May 12, 2012** *So much I learned from Maureen's life and her death. There is no going back; there is only going forward.* **So I might as well get around to loving my body as it is. It never ceased to be the temple of the Holy Spirit.**

Visitors sometimes asked Karis how she managed to maintain her smile and sweet spirit and concern for other people through all she had to endure. She said, "Every morning before I open my eyes I say 'Help, Lord!—I can't do this by myself!' and he gives me what I need, his manna for this one day."

> **Jun 4, 2012** *Yesterday I chose not to go to church, too weary to face the disappointment if You weren't there or to handle it if You were. I wanted not to be with people but have You to myself. I haven't been home or alone at all for far too long and it finally caught up with me: grieving for Lacie and Maureen; worrying about Gary and Carissa, screaming to have Lacie's perky, bubbly self back. Screaming for Karen, too, or more for Michael whom she left behind. Screaming for all my Beloveds.*

> **Jun 15, 2012** *"25% more free" announces the Planters peanut bottle from my dresser. "It's mocking me," I think back. "You've got to be*

kidding." Is it possible to be 25% more free? Well, perhaps I am. I can walk now. I can get up from my bed. I can't get up and just walk around on my own or people will freak out. Even if they didn't, they hook me up to a pole so that half of my life I live on a leash.

But the freedom is there. Enough. And I thank You for it. I pray for joy and strength and courage that come only from Your Presence. I say this every morning, toward the patch of sky out my window.

A few days later our world twisted again. Dr. K would be leaving Pittsburgh.

Jun 20, 2012 Summer Solstice *I received a letter yesterday informing me that Dr. K will be leaving, going to Cleveland Clinic. You have lent a certain portion of Your glory to this man—Your insight, Your self-gift, Your righteous anger, Your affection—and he will be sorely missed. Your mystery, Your illogical thinking, Your perfume.*

Lord, thank You for planting hints of Yourself everywhere. For the great adventure and privilege it has been to touch this man. To have him as a surgeon, to have personally walked with one of the greats.

As kidney stress took its toll, making Karis weary and confused, she said to me, "Mom, do you miss me? Because I miss me. I can't find myself."

Jul 22, 2012 *For the absence of myself: that is why I told Mom and Dad I am distressed right now. There is no lack of security or choice or pleasure or people who are gentle with me and who seem to like me. There is no lack but of energy and motivation and courage and joy. Lord, rejuvenate me and sustain me. Love us all, Father—hold us; do not venture us more than we can bear. Tease us away from worry and yet also from foolhardiness. Please, Lord, restore my mind someday.*

August 24, celebrating two and a half weeks of no clinic and no hospital, Dr. C told Karis it was time to start preparing medically for her November trip to Brazil for Valerie's wedding.

Aug 31, 2012 *Val's wedding invitations are spread out on the coffee table in front of me, awaiting bows and addresses and stuffing into envelopes. I am realizing that no one expects me to get off TPN before my trip to Brazil for the wedding week.*

Last night, by Your grace, I went to Arabic Fellowship even though everything in my body was crying not to, a place where we worship in Spirit and Truth. Thank You, thank You, thank You.

Oct 3, 2012 *Today I am in the "mustashfaa"* [hospital] *again with pneumonia, a pleural effusion, and dehydration. I'm going to miss Laurelville* [our annual church retreat], *Vera's first art exposé, Jonah's Call, Café Mona with Martha, a dermatology appointment, PT wellness program, Music History class, small group, Arabic Fellowship . . . **I feel as though everything is shifting. I come back to what I know: You are to be feared. You are creating a story that is larger than any of us**.*

October 17-31, my sister Jan cared for Karis while I spent two weeks in Brazil for the launching of the new edition of my book for sexual abuse survivors. After my return, I would have less than two weeks to prepare a myriad of details for taking Karis to Brazil November 12 for Valerie's wedding the 17th.

A week before we were to leave, these cherished plans fell apart. Karis had an accident with her aide that ruptured a vein in her right thigh. By the time we reached the ER, her thigh was enormous and her hemoglobin was 5 (normal is 12-15.5). Karis lost (internally) over half the blood in her body. The pain in her hugely swollen thigh was intolerable.

Shattered. The word is not too dramatic. Karis described missing Valerie's wedding as "the biggest disappointment of my life." Her nurses grieved with her. But one day the head nurse on the transplant floor had an idea: she would "host" Valerie's wedding at the hospital through live streaming from Brazil! Jan, who rearranged her plans to stay on with Karis while I was away, described this on the blog:

I was intercepted by Marcia, the 12N Nursing Coordinator calling herself the "wedding planner," as I arrived at the hospital this morning with "wedding-watching" clothes for Karis. Marcia, the doctors and hospital staff are really excited about this, and here's what they've done:

The Montefiore auditorium (with a big screen) on the 7th floor is reserved for us Saturday from 2-4 pm. The hospital is providing a catered buffet, wedding cake, coffee, and punch. Marcia is helping me invite people from 11N, 12N, the Transplant ICU and the Transplant Clinic, in addition to our Pittsburgh-area friends. Hospital technicians have already contacted Valerie's fiancé in Brazil for a trial Skype contact.

We were blown away by Marcia and the hospital's generosity and creativity. The event was a huge success. No, it wasn't the same for Karis as being there. Valerie talked with her just before walking down the aisle, and knew she was trying hard to keep her chin up. But what extravagant kindness!

When I returned to Pittsburgh November 20, Dr. C decided to double Karis's pain coverage so she would be able to tolerate getting up and walking, essential to preventing pneumonia as her leg slowly healed. Karis longed for home. December 8 she got her way. December 12 my mother died after more than twenty years with Alzheimer's. Dave planned to stay home while I attended the memorial service, but Karis said, "I AM going." And the trip went well, portable oxygen and all.

We celebrated Christmas at home, saddened by the death of our transplant friend Hans. Karis welcomed 2013 with a wonderful new aide, A, to brighten her life.

Jan 30, 2013 *Today I got to take a shower, and laugh in the car with A, and she fixed me mint tea. Yesterday A read to me from A Thousand Gifts. Today she exercised and stretched my feet. There was rain, and baby pictures, and warmth, and reminders to laugh at myself and live in the moment.*

Feb 10, 2013 *I remembered today Your embrace, Lord. **Your body bearing the same wounds as mine**. I remember the ways You have guided and protected me all the days of my life. You have given me insight and peace. You have given me awesome gifts, and through me amazing gifts to others. Thank You.*

From March on, Karis was in and out of the hospital every few weeks. Our aide A stuck with us through months of erratic paychecks—when Karis was hospitalized, A couldn't work, so wasn't paid.

A delightful break at our friends' cabin in the woods

Mar 13, 2013 *Outside the sky is silver, and it is snowing. We are back from our family weekend at Glade Spring and at the hospital with fever* *and high kidney numbers. Mama and I had to come back early from a wonderful time of walking around the lake, playing games, sitting by the fireplace, watching Hogan's Heroes and Princess Bride, eating marvelous meals, making puzzles, playing soccer in mud and slush, feeding the birds . . . They said the stars were breathtaking.*

I got to know Brian [Rachel's boyfriend] *a lot better; spent time interrogating him. I was so constantly needy I couldn't see how he could stand me, but his text messages afterwards indicated that he had a genuinely good time. What do I think of him? Wow. He has a servant's heart, a thoughtful instinct, a generous spirit. He is affectionate. He is more traveled than Rachel herself, but does not want to move to Brazil—Rachel seems to be accepting that, but will she really be happy in the U.S.?*

Even with all that was going on with her, God gave Karis opportunities to reach out.

Apr 28, 2013 Montefiore *Josh, an intern here on 11 North, just asked me to pray for him, and that led to a long conversation. Lord, help him to understand my words, that You are with us, dwelling among us, knowing our sufferings.*

April 29 renal doctors told us Karis had 18 percent kidney function and perhaps six months to live. Neither dialysis nor kidney transplant were possible because she had no possible venous access in addition to the line in her neck, which was dedicated to TPN.

Six months to live? The idea emboldened Karis. If she had only this much more time on planet Earth, she must make the most of it! She tested her limits outrageously, from the perspective of friends who just wanted her to be safe. She said, "How can I know what I can't do if I don't try?"

By testing her limits, Karis created memories. She focused more on the feeling of stretching to reach something on a high shelf than on the split leg that resulted as she lost her balance; on her desire to let me sleep than on the fall when she got up at night by herself; on her sense of freedom while walking home alone from PT instead of the disappointment of having to call me to rescue her.

Rediscovering the six-months-to-live question in Karis's journal lit a fire under me to write this book. It feels, oddly, like the one thing *I* have to do before I die.

> **May 2, 2013** *Three days to the end of my twenties. May 5 falls on a Sunday this year. I have not wanted to make plans involving other people, because it would be a huge disappointing hassle for everyone were they to fall through.*

For her thirtieth birthday, Karis requested a perennial garden, planted with cuttings from the gardens of friends, and a birdfeeder she could see from her recliner. Karis began calling this her "Friendship Garden." Her friend Georges rototilled part of our back yard, and people began arriving to plant their flowers. Sometimes, eating dinner, we noticed out the window someone walking into our back yard bearing plants and garden tools. Each bloom became a reminder of someone's love and generosity.

> **Jun 9, 2013** ***God, let's DO something!*** *I have been isolating myself and living in a small, narrow world. Most of my plans now are only in my head. I am indebted to so many, not only for gifts and money and ears and prayers and food, but genuine love. I want to give back happiness and actions that flow from Your Spirit, but everything I try seems not to work out. I am a grounded albatross.*

In June 2013, I received a surprise call from Karis's former dean at Notre Dame. Karis's professors and the honors program director had decided to send her diploma, which had been held all this time awaiting the final version of her thesis. Several profs, the dean told me, considered Karis one of the brightest students they had ever taught. Karis was grateful, but as she had been her senior year of high school, was deeply disappointed in her inability to complete the work to her own satisfaction.

June 15, a renal doctor spent a long time with us explaining Karis's kidney situation. His bottom line was that she might have a year to live.

A year? For Karis, this prognosis felt like moving the finish line mid-race. Since the six-month projection at the end of April she had internally programmed herself to say good-bye to family and friends at Thanksgiving. How could she keep going even longer?

Jun 17, 2013 *Lord, tonight Daddy held me while I soaked his shirt with mucus and tears, until 2:30 in the morning. He told me he saw three possible purposes to my life: helping people find and believe in their dreams, prayer, and poetry.*

I want to scream and yell and dance around throwing a temper tantrum. Because Dad's words are so close to comforting me. And my wound is as deep as the sea. It should not be comforted. It burns like crud. Acid on my skin. I hate people who accept me as lost forever, as less forever.

Forgive my pride in imagining Daddy's dreams for me too small: if I could accomplish them, truly, it would be more than enough.

Jun 18, 2013 *I awoke this morning somehow purified. Simple. Daddy and I went out into the puddly garden—I fell once but he caught me. I craned my neck to see the flowers, bedraggled and wind-lashed and water-heavy. I could have lingered in the garden forever, had I been strong, had I not been already late for 7 West. Mama planted all the tomatoes together, and the raspberries as a cluster too. The hostas are blooming, as well as the roses.*

Thank You for my father, who sat and held me into the wee hours before traveling to Paraguay this morning. I didn't realize that upon arrival in Asunción he is to be shuttled straight to the conference. Nor that he had yet to pack. But he stayed up with me anyway, letting me take my time, nudging me with questions and encouragements until I managed to express a small bit of what I was feeling.

Jul 3, 2013 *A week until Ramadan. Five days until Val's arrival. My first day off of visiting 7 West madrugally* [early mornings] *for eight weeks straight. Dad's home from Brazil; we went to the Heinz History Museum. Alan's yellow flowers are blooming; new grass planted around* *the holly, the fence fixed, a riot of wildflowers emerging. We cooked with our own fresh basil and parsley.*

My heart-cry, "God, let's DO something!" *slowly appears to be more of a possibility. I'm in charge of arts and crafts for the family reunion.*

Valerie and Cesar came from Brazil for an Elliott extended family reunion July 11-15, of the eight of us siblings and our families (about fifty of us). Karis's friend Larissa went with us to help with her care so that I could spend more time with family members I seldom saw. Karis's goal was to interact personally and individually with each one of her cousins. She didn't expect to see most of them again.

Cesar and Valerie took Karis canoeing at our family reunion—pure delight!

Jul 27, 2013 *Lord, I remember again the vision of You when You opened Your arms to me in my uncleanness, **my scars on Your body**. I have wanted so much to be Your servant, as if that were in a way more dignified, more worthy. I have wanted it so much. But You say to me, I have called You by name, "Daughter." I don't deserve it. Not anything. You have shown me grace. Shame and fear and grace. **Your power, made perfect in weakness; Your grace sufficient.***

__Show me which are Your promises and what is my imagination and where they meet__. Oh, to be with You! To have accomplished through You everything You intended for me. I look forward to that day more than any other—when we can be together. But I continue with my child's heart cry, Papa: "Let's DO something!" Like little Val used to say to me when she climbed up on my bed in São Paulo.

Aug 18, 2013 *You hold me together, Papa, body to soul, with the prayers of the saints. **You have tucked my mind into Your mind.** You tell me I don't need one thing more than Your grace. **You will use me for the nations.** You surround me with three angels: one to protect, one to comfort, one to guide. You call Yourself Emmanuel, God with us. Our refuge and our strength. "I am with you."*

For the third time (I think) in all the years we lived in Pittsburgh, Karis was well enough to attend our annual church retreat at Laurelville. On our way there, we received the sad news that our transplant friend Julie had died. Karis was grateful to have visited her and said good-bye before we left.

Oct 8, 2013 *All the time at Laurelville people were telling me about my smile—how my very expression communicates something of You, Lord. I have been blessed by blessing people, even when my mind was not entirely intact. Your Spirit of love was there. I felt full of manna.*

October 10, Karis had an accident that cost us our beloved aide A. Karis, brazenly testing her limits, fell on a treadmill. Copious bleeding—panic—911—ambulance . . . A couldn't handle seeing Karis get so hurt under her care.

We had planned a garden party for Saturday, October 12, to honor those who contributed to Karis's friendship garden. We had already postponed twice, once in August and once in September. Karis told her doctor this time, "I AM going," and indeed, fortified by pain medication, she arrived at her party only about an hour late, cheerfully greeting her guests as though perfectly fine. God graced us with a warm, bright day for October, and though the garden was no longer at its peak, it was still beautiful. For Karis, the "flowers" that mattered most were the friends who had created the garden for her.

At the party, we planted a fruit cocktail tree, purchased by Karis after extensive research. Karis explained that as the different fruits (apricot, plum, nectarine, and peach) had been grafted into one tree, so friends' love has been grafted into her, producing a variety of fruits in her life. As well, the little tree honored her donors, whose organs were grafted into her body. The tree is flourishing and we eat its fruit with joy, remembering the generous friends who gathered in our garden that day.

As the weather grew colder, we had difficulty keeping Karis warm. She had lost a great deal of weight, and didn't seem able to moderate her own body temperature. Increased fatigue and higher levels of ammonia in her blood caused confusion and difficulty expressing herself, but still she journaled.

> **Nov 22, 2013** *Before birth I was flung upon You, Lord. You were always my portion, my inheritance; I was sustained by Your hand and the church and my family. By miracle after miracle, hard work and insight and sacrifice and timing and scientific innovation I have remained on Earth, spirit linked with body for these 30 years.*
>
> *I have been privileged to live a full life. So many joyous memories and so much love surround me. Travels and loves, hopes and promises, living always with the Mystery of You. Deep losses, sorrows, ways in which I have disappointed or damaged people. Learning things the hard way and the easy way. Like Frodo the Hobbit coming to today with no glory of my own, stretched thin, not beginning to comprehend, rummaging in the dark for Your voice, for the next step.*

*Lord, You love memory . . . yet You have taken it from me. And words. And faithfulness. And joy. My dreams of being a translator, a doctor, of having a husband and a daughter, **of having a ministry among the nations, finding the key**: should I abandon them? Some, all, none?*

What does "seu amado está guardado" mean, if I never marry? Could I have misinterpreted? Did You mean, for example, that Anthony's soul was guarded—through my daily prayers for him? Is this a cop-out or lack of faith? Or is this what You intended and envisioned all along?!

December 16-19 we were honored by a visit from our pastor, Vandeir, and his wife Hildete from our church in São Paulo! This was a very significant time for Karis. She gave Pastor Vandeir the gift of a tiny stuffed lamb, telling him she had always been his "sheep." Hildete "slept" on the floor of Karis's room one night, and they talked the night away, about pain, how to prepare for death, how to understand the promise and the prophecy.

Dec 17, 2013 *My Lord and my God, my Guidance and my Deliverance, I believe You have said, and have actually given me, freedom from pain. I have victory over it. A gift, from You.*

But not freedom from feeling pain. Let me explain, so that whoever comes to read this one day won't misunderstand. You said we are servants and slaves to whatever rules us. If we are submitted to You, we are Your servants—the most free people on Earth, submitted rightly to our Creator, the All-Knower, who knows how we fit together and what is best for us. We fear You and You alone.

But I had come to fear pain. I didn't want it anymore. So I behaved as if You were not going to protect my soul and spirit: I avoided pain.

When You freed me from pain the other night, You didn't stop the pain itself. You just set my fears straight, so I would realize I did not need to live enslaved by pain. The only one I should fear is You. So now I can live without pain medicine to the point I can handle it. I can tolerate a lot more because I know what I want and what I want is a clear mind.

But I also have the freedom to take pain medicine when things get unbearable. It's not the pain medicine in and of itself that is good or evil; it's the dominion I let it have over me.

Right now I can take some pain medicine and sleep well, but have nightmares. And wake up in the middle of the night wanting more. And I would be confused and further damage my mind. Or I can refuse pain medicine, and have a difficult night. I would feel every bit of the pain, sleep in starts, wake up disgruntled, have trouble getting out of bed, need to sleep during the day.

Either way I am not sinning. Pain doesn't reign over me, whether it's there or not there. I think tonight I will choose to go without. Thank You for this freedom.

December 20 Dave's mother died peacefully while her son Bill was visiting her from England. The timing was amazing: the extended Kornfield clan had already gathered in Pittsburgh for an early Christmas before the focus shifted to cousin Sarah's wedding. We were able to have our own memorial service for Abuelita, sharing stories and memories, before Karis had to be admitted to the hospital December 23 with dehydration. The official memorial service was scheduled for Florida January 13.

When Karis was discharged December 31, Dr. C requested we ask everyone we knew to pray for a breakthrough for Karis. I wrote: "What's really great is that Karis feels better after this hospitalization than she has for a long time! Such a nice way to end the year and look toward a new one."

As was our family custom, we welcomed 2014 sharing the verses each of us selected for the New Year. Karis chose Mark 5:41, "He took her by the hand and said to her, 'Talitha cum,' which means, 'Little girl, get up!'" Karis told us she had been discouraged, but God was telling her to rouse herself and stop her "pity party" (her words). If God had more months of life for her, she wanted to live them well.

Jan 7, 2014 *I told Valerie about my new joy, my re-establishment in hope. Yes, Val is here—she arrived yesterday, Feast of the Kings, the last day of Christmas, Epiphany.*

We had asked Valerie to come from Brazil for her January summer vacation month to care for Karis while Dave and I hosted four Brazilian couples in Orlando, Florida. We hoped to take Valerie and Karis with us, and much of my time during the early days of January was spent preparing for that trip.

I wrote on Karis's blog January 11, 2014, the eighth anniversary of Karis's second transplant:

> Monday the final decision will be made about whether Karis can go with us to Florida for a few days. If the answer is yes, we will fly early Tuesday. On this transplant anniversary, please be encouraged with us.

Once again, though, Karis's roller coaster took a twist we did not anticipate.

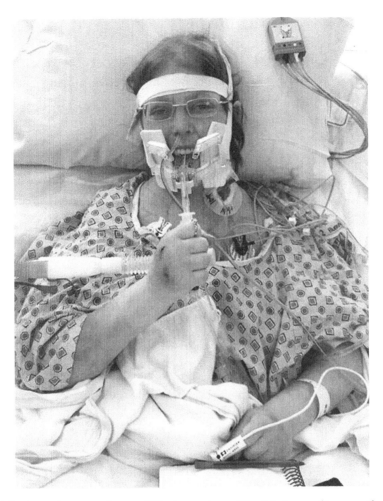

The last photo we have of Karis awake: still with her radiant smile!

CHAPTER 20

Father, Take Me Home

Age Thirty
January 13-February 5, 2014
Montefiore Hospital

Day 1, Monday, January 13, 2014

Karis grinned as we prepped for her check-up. Today the doctors would approve her trip to Florida! For weeks we had been planning for this event. We had the brilliant idea of bringing Karis's little sis Valerie from Brazil to accompany Karis while Dave and I hosted four pastor couples from Brazil. Top on Karis's wish list was Sea World. She had always loved all things marine.

After a battery of exams at 7 West, three different doctors high-fived Karis, declaring her fit to travel. Val did a celebratory dance and we headed home to last-minute packing and errands. We would fly to Orlando the next morning.

When we untangled Karis from her treasured new coat (her brother Dan's Christmas gift) and settled her on the couch for a nap, she pulled my head down and whispered, "Mama, I'm not feeling very well."

"It's probably all the excitement," I said, tucking her electric throw around her, chafing her hands to warm them from the outdoor cold. "Relax and sleep while I shop for the last things we need." Val set to work counting out and packing medical supplies into duffle bags, and I ran out the door.

Back home, chilled to the bone, one look at Karis told me she was not going to Florida. The flush on her cheeks was fever. I called the doctor. He had just been informed by the lab that Karis was septic.

Valerie and I sat by Karis's bed in the ICU watching antibiotics drip into her veins as life-saving medications gradually restored her bottomed-out blood pressure. Chills swept over us. What if symptoms had shown up only AFTER we had boarded the plane to Florida?! It didn't bear thinking about.

Day 2, Tuesday, January 14, 2014

Our flight to Florida cancelled, Valerie and I showed up at the ICU on the first stroke of visiting hours. The routine was familiar, yet always carried inherent anxiety. How had Karis fared through the night? The nurses didn't appreciate being pestered for information before the 7:00 am change of shift. But the news was good—Karis had stabilized and the docs were already talking about transferring her out of ICU to the floor!

Karis's doctor encouraged me to join Dave in Florida. "You know the drill. We'll switch out her contaminated central line and then send her up to 11 North. A few more days on antibiotics, and she'll be fine. Valerie is the best medicine she could have. Get out of here, and let your girls enjoy each other!"

I rebooked a flight for that afternoon. Rachel would be by to see Karis right after her class at the University of Pittsburgh. Dan called from DC, confirming Karis was OK before he caught a flight to Mexico for consultant work. As I left for the bus to the airport, Val and Karis were chattering away in Portuguese, hardly pausing for my good-bye hugs. "No worries, Mama, we'll be fine!"

On the plane, I was overwhelmed by God's mercy in protecting Karis from traveling with me. Without emergency critical care, she could have died within hours of the first symptoms of infection in her bloodstream.

Brushing away the feeling that I should not be leaving Karis, I wondered how Dave's mom's memorial service had gone the day before. Dave and his sister Kathy from Bolivia had organized it. Today Dave was rushing to prepare for the arrival of our friends from Brazil. I chuckled, realizing I had Val's birthday gift in my suitcase. It was par for the course: how often we had celebrated birthdays and holidays in the hospital!

Day 3, Wednesday, January 15, 2014

"My job now is not to worry about Karis. Karis is fine." I reminded myself of this several times a day as Dave and I laughed and played with the four Brazilian couples who were so excited to see Disney World and Epcot.

"Karis is doing well," Valerie assured me on the phone. "Enjoy everything so you can tell us all about it!"

I had to smile, thinking about the special memories the girls would be making together while I was gone. I purposed—again—to focus on finding everything I could to be thankful for, to silence the niggling worry at the back of my mind.

I started thinking about times God had intervened that were so spectacular we would never forget:

Kick-starting her intestine at six weeks when the doctors said she should die.

Giving her life back through the surgery Dr. P performed in Detroit when she was three. "Mommy, nothing hurts!"

Showing us through biopsies at age 11 that there was no possibility Karis's intestine could function: Every good day was a miracle!

Saving her life when she was 16, when her fever went off the end of the thermometer and the nurse was too frightened to act.

Saving her life after her first transplant through the only person who could recognize Legionella early enough to obtain the right medications.

Keeping her alive through an impossible surgery to remove her disintegrating graft while Legionnaire's ravaged her lungs.

Bringing her through 74 days of coma and weaning from the ventilator—the sickest patient ever to leave the Pittsburgh Children's Hospital ICU alive.

Keeping her with us through her second, five-organ transplant, and the fifty days of ICU after that, and the rejection that stripped her intestine after her surgery in 2009, and the sepsis which followed . . .

Day 4, Thursday, January 16, 2014

"Sweetheart, your voice sounds a little hoarse. Do you have a sore throat?"

"Yeah, I seem to have picked up a cold. But no worries—the doctor already looked at my throat. It's a little red but nothing alarming. Today Val and I are going to play Boggle and several friends are coming over to visit. We're having a great time. Don't worry about a measly little cold—I'm not."

This was typical Karis, focusing on LIFE rather than worrying about her health. This wasn't just a little cold, though—by the end of the day Karis required oxygen and was diagnosed with pneumonia.

Still she was upbeat, talking about the fun she was having with friends who had come to visit her. She had quickly laid aside her disappointment over the aborted vacation trip to Florida. She described the kindness of a nurse, a joke with a friend, beating her sisters at word games. . . .

I remembered a line from a poem Karis wrote when she was nine: "Oh, every bit of sadness is much smaller than my gladness."

Karis habitually chose to find gladness where others would only have seen sadness; to find God's love where others would have felt ill-treated. Because of those choices, she found strength in the midst of her struggles. Her smile, her joy, her love and concern for others—these traits had endeared her to us and to all who knew her.

Yes, I was tired from the 24/7 care Karis required. This vacation was very welcome. But what a privilege had been mine, to care for this daughter through her ups and downs for thirty years.

I was jerked out of my thankful reverie by friends yelling "Débora, finalmente chegamos ao fim da fila! Vamos entrar!" (Finally we've reached the end of the line! It's time to go in!) And soon I was caught up in my friends' conversations and the "Circle of Life" film at Epcot.

Day 5, Friday, January 17, 2014

The word "pneumonia" pushed all my mommy-worry buttons, despite the girls saying "No, no, you don't need to come back. We're fine! Enjoy your vacation!"

For me, that was easier said than done. I had too many pneumonia-memories: long, weary, terrifying days in the ICU, comas with no idea what might be going on in Karis' soul, days of speaking every word of comfort I could give, when she couldn't speak back to me, days and nights when her every breath was controlled by a machine with a tube down her throat.

I knew this pneumonia had been caught early, that Karis was already on antibiotics, that so far her symptoms were not "serious." But too many times I had seen things go very badly very quickly . . .

I put on a happy face for the sake of our friends, but my heart was with my girls at Montefiore Hospital. "Lord, help Karis! Help me!" And he did. He sent angels to Montefiore. It would be some time yet before I read Karis' last journal entry, but on this day, January 17, Karis wrote, "Thank you, Father, for the angels. I've decided to call them Faith, Hope, and Love."

All praise and thanks to you, my Lord!

Day 6, Saturday, January 18, 2014—Valerie's Birthday

In Valerie's words:

My birthday came at the end of a week with Karis in the hospital while Mom and Dad were in Florida. What a week it was! Scrabble games, walks, great talks, such a special time just with Karis. I remember Karis's love and concern for me that week, about how I was dealing with our decision to move to the United States, missing Brazil, missing Cesar, asking her nurse for a "fronha" instead of a pillowcase . . . my internal battle displayed in semantics. Karis told me I should be easier on myself. She helped me rest. Even though she was the "patient," my big sister cared for me.

On my birthday, we had a fun morning--washing hair, painting nails, using the glittery polish Karis gave me for Christmas. She "bought" me birthday balloons (I went down to the gift shop to get them). In the evening, Rachel, Brian, and Larissa joined us. We shared a delicious cake, gifts, songs, played skipbo . . . Karis watched "Oppa Gangnam Style" and "What does the fox say" with a somewhat horrified expression on her face. . .

What a gift what precious days we had together, after being apart for so long.

The ICU nurses said I look like Karis, that I have her smile. I am so thankful for her prayers and encouragement each step of the way, as I learned to walk, to swim, to write, to read, to sing, to dance. . . to be a nurse. . . so thankful that she helped make me the person I am.

Day 7, Sunday, January 19, 2014

On this Lord's Day, Karis's symptoms worsened.

At 10:30 pm, our friend Larissa called me. "I spent the evening with Karis. I'm going home now, but very reluctantly. She's not doing well, and the nurses aren't taking it seriously. At my insistence, they called the resident, but he didn't seem very concerned. I just wanted you to know that I'm worried about her."

I called Karis's nurse. "Yes, your friend was quite alarmed. I'll keep an eye on her, and promise I'll call you if anything changes. We just need to give the antibiotics time to work. You know Karis—she'll be OK. She always beats the odds."

I knew there were no flights to Pittsburgh until morning, but I checked anyway, just in case.

Midnight: Give all your worries and cares to God, for he cares about you.

1:15 a.m.: Give all your worries and cares to God, for he cares about you.

2:47 a.m.: Give all your worries and cares to God, for he cares about you.

3:23 a.m.: Give all your worries and cares to God, for he cares about you . . .

4:30 a.m.: My cell phone rang.

Day 8, Monday, January 20, 2014

Now Karis's nurse was concerned. "We've used all our resources to increase Karis's oxygenation, but we're not holding her above 77 percent. Would you like to speak with her before we go down to the ICU?"

Karis could barely talk, gasping for breath. "Mama, please come."

"I'll be on the next flight. Go now, and may the Lord give you his peace."

The thought crossed Dave's mind that he should go with me. But he felt a responsibility to our Brazilian guests. He had two more days with them.

While I waited to board my plane, Val called from ICU. Karis was doing well on 60 percent oxygen via BiPAP (non-invasive ventilation). That was good news indeed. She had not required the ventilator. I made the trip much more at ease.

When I arrived, Karis was resting quietly, with the BiPAP now down to 50 percent. Perhaps those antibiotics were kicking in! Why then was she running a fever?

Give all your worries and cares to God . . .

Day 9, Tuesday, January 21, 2014

Blog post:

> It's a beautiful snowy morning in Pittsburgh. Karis had a good night, but this morning her chest x-ray is worse and she is very tired from breathing through the bipap. The ICU doc just came by to say she'll be placed on a ventilator to help heal the pneumonia. Here's a word of encouragement: *The Lord himself watches over you* (Psalm 121:5).

Later (noon):

> Karis is being intubated right now. Her arterial blood gas came back 67. Everyone hopes it will be just for a couple of days. The pneumonia is consolidated now in both lungs. The ventilator will allow her body to rest and devote all its energy to healing. They wanted to do a bronchoscopy as they intubated Karis, but didn't have a small enough caliber bronchoscopy set. Valerie and I sang Karis to sleep with Brazilian worship songs.

Day 10, Wednesday, January 22, 2014

Blog post:

> When I walked in this morning, I was surprised by Karis's smile and bright eyes, through and around all the tubes and tape. She was sitting up in bed, fully awake! They've let up on the sedation (obviously!) and have brought her oxygen down to 50%. They tried to let her breathe on her own but she quickly got too tired, so she's back on a rate controlled by the vent and is more relaxed now.

> She's been communicating with us by writing on a paper, but that's challenging because her right hand is extremely swollen and painful and she's *not* ambidextrous.

Dr. C thinks both lungs look better. We appreciated a visit from one of the pastors of our church this morning, grateful that Karis was awake and able to participate in the conversation and prayers.

Day 11, Thursday, January 23, 2014

Blog post:

> A bit of confusion this morning: Karis was trying to turn over in bed and dislodged the breathing tube. Rather than reposition it, they removed it and put her back on BiPap. But she's working really hard to breathe and is exhausted, so now they're intubating again, and are going to sedate her a little more so she can rest better. Her x-ray hasn't improved, so while they intubate they'll perform a bronchoscopy with a set from the children's hospital, to culture a sample from her lungs. Our group in Florida is dispersing today and Dave will be home tonight.

Karis wrote laboriously with her left hand, "I love you, Mom. I love you, Val. I love Dad, I love Dan, I love Rachel, I love Brian, I love Cesar, I love Larissa." Then, "Call the doctor. I CAN'T BREATHE."

Just as I turned to alert the nurse, the doctor walked in saying "Karis, your oxygenation is too low. We're going to have to intubate and sedate you again. I showed him what Karis had written and he nodded, asking us to leave the room so they could act quickly. Karis gave us a brilliant smile as they started lowering her head and the room filled with nurses and therapists. That was her last communication with Val and me.

Did Karis know? Did she write out all the "I love you's" as her final gift to us (along with that smile)?

Day 12, Friday, January 24, 2014

Dave came straight to the hospital from the airport Thursday night and was able to see Karis for a few minutes before visiting hours ended. He said she squeezed his hand a bit and her eyelashes fluttered. He was quite sure she heard him and knew he was there. I was so glad.

Dr. C kept telling us we just needed to give the antibiotics time to work, but she had been on high-power antibiotics for more than a week already. If there was not a change for the better by the next day, they would consult Infectious Diseases.

> O God of peace, who has taught us that in returning and rest we shall be saved, in quietness and in confidence shall be our strength: By the might of your Spirit lift us, we pray, to your presence, where we may be still and know that you are God; through Jesus Christ our Lord, Amen.

Day 13, Saturday, January 25, 2014

The Infectious Diseases doctor walked in with a nose swab in her hand, saying Karis had not been checked for H1N1 upon admission.

What?! How could it be possible that such a simple, routine procedure was missed—not just once, but three times: when she was first admitted to the ICU with sepsis, when she was admitted to 11N, and again when she was transferred back to the ICU in respiratory distress!

I asked Dr. S about this later, when the swine flu results came back positive. He said my question—how the routine nose swab had fallen through the cracks—was the main topic of conversation for the whole transplant team. They were devastated that they had missed the correct diagnosis.

Karis did not have bacterial pneumonia; she had H1N1, or "swine flu" as it is popularly known. No wonder she was not responding to all the high-power antibiotics! They started a high dose of oral TamiFlu without much confidence that she would absorb it, since her intestine by now was not functioning at all. The ID doc put in a request to the FDA for Karis to receive an experimental IV form of flu antivirus, the only IV medication of its kind.

The ICU limited visitors to "family only," and each of us had to observe strict protocol for gowning, masking, and gloving while we were with Karis—for our own protection and to prevent the spread of the virus to others, especially the other vulnerable patients in the ICU.

The H1N1 diagnosis was not good news, but at least we finally knew what Karis was dealing with—and why she had not been getting better.

The entries that follow, written in present tense, are from my own journal.

Day 14, Sunday, January 26, 2014

"It's too soon to see any improvement," says the Infectious Diseases doctor. Karis is hanging in there, but her ventilator settings have been increased twice today.

On this Lord's Day, we know that prayers are being offered for Karis in many places around the world. It is humbling to think of so many people caring about our little girl and her struggle to survive this day. Thank you, Lord. May your will be done on earth as it is in heaven.

Thank you for Church of the Ascension. Today an announcement is being made that only family may visit Karis, but that friends may come to the ICU waiting room to spend time and pray with us. Many people have brought us food and other types of practical encouragement. How good God has been in every phase of Karis's life to give her—and us—strong support in each place she has lived: Wheaton, IL; Port Huron, MI; São Paulo, Brazil; South Bend, IN; and Pittsburgh, PA. Her life has been so rich in loving relationships.

> O God, you manifest in your servants the signs of your presence;
> Send forth upon us the Spirit of love, that in companionship with
> one another your abounding grace may increase among us; through
> Jesus Christ our Lord. Amen.

Day 15, Monday, January 27, 2014

The FDA has approved IV antiviral medication for Karis. It should arrive in time for her to receive her first dose this afternoon. The Infectious Diseases doc tells me that the Tamiflu has not had a noticeable impact (except negatively on her kidneys); Karis' H1N1 virus load is still high. We hope the IV medication will be more effective, but we may not see significant improvement for a week to ten days.

As I spend hours beside Karis watching her "sleep," I am grateful that she can't see herself right now. Karis always had a streak of vanity. She was deeply distressed by "what she had become" (as she said) as a result of long-term steroids and the impact of her illness.

Now, Karis's face and body are swollen because her kidneys aren't functioning well enough to filter fluid from her blood. Tape on her nose holds an NG tube in place. The breathing tube down her throat is secured by more tape, and by bands that wind around her head. We have given up trying to keep her hair straightened under these bands. The pulse oximeter on her finger, multiple IV and arterial lines, and the wires that monitor her heart easily tangle with one another. I remove the blood pressure cuff whenever I can for a few minutes of relief for her arm.

As I help the nurses bathe Karis, I trace the multiplicity of scars all over her body, from surgeries and from falls. Each one tells a story of crisis and of healing. How many, many battles this girl has fought! How many times she scrabbled her way back to a level of stability, only to get knocked down again.

Few people, I muse, have any idea of the courage it has taken for this girl to keep on believing in life, keep on dealing with whatever any given day threw at her, keep on loving God and the people around her, keep on trusting that God would keep her on this earth exactly as long as he had use for her here.

This bruised, battle-weary girl's beauty is stunning.

Day 16, Tuesday, January 28, 2014

I have time, as I sit for hours beside her bed, to think about the adventurous life Karis has led. Who knew that this girl, who was not supposed to survive infancy, would become a world traveler, fascinated with cultures and peoples from all parts of our complex world?

Who knew that she would become a "time traveler," delving for knowledge deep in the past, soaking in the words of wise and famous people whom she heard speak at Notre Dame. And peering into the future for people she was passionately concerned for: boy soldiers in Myanmar, children born with AIDS in Africa, slum and street children in the cities of Brazil, children trapped in the violence of the Middle East, women without voice in every part of the world, even in America.

Karis so longed to make a difference in the lives of people who suffered, no matter where they were or what circumstances bound them.

David called Karis a "bridge person," someone who could understand multiple points of view and help people hear each other. Karis bridged America and Latin America, Protestant and Catholic, white and black, Asian, African, and European. She bridged old and young, rich and poor, those educated formally and those with street smarts.

She was equally comfortable chatting with a custodian and with the Archbishop of Nigeria. She befriended people who were physically ill, mentally ill, and emotionally ill, understanding from the inside out that pain is pain.

Karis was a people-magnet. I don't believe this was all rooted just in her personality. She prayed from the time she was young, *"Lord, use me somehow to love your people. Love people through me."* God answered those prayers.

What a wonder that I had been privileged to walk beside this girl, this bridge-builder, this adventurer, this lover of the world and its people, this curious, insatiable learner about God's creation, both animate and inanimate.

I am grateful, Lord. You have walked with us through all of the adventures—all of the twists and turns of Karis' roller coaster, even in the dark. I thank you.

Day 17, Wednesday, January 29, 2014

The doctors and respiratory therapists decided to turn Karis onto her stomach. I remembered that when she was in her pneumonia coma in December 2004, this maneuver helped her breathe better for a while. It's a complex thing to accomplish, with all the lines and tubes protruding from her body that have to be individually repositioned.

I was not prepared for how difficult it was to turn Karis herself. As gentle as the nurses were, Karis suffered two skin tears. One was stitch-able and one was not: they just let it bleed, changing the dressing from time to time.

Turning her did raise her blood pressure slightly, to 90/52. But to everyone's disappointment, all this effort did not noticeably improve her respiratory stats. She still breathed at 88 percent, despite high levels of oxygen and pressure from the respirator.

Our comic relief of the day: When I thanked the respiratory therapist for his work, he said, "I'm from West Virginia. I know how to make the monkeys play together."

???

Obviously, we are not conversant with West Virginian monkeys!

God, how much more can this tortured body take? How much more can *we* take?

What do you want of us?

Day 18, Thursday, January 30, 2014

Blog post by Rachel:

> We have a lovely nurse today. The ICU and transplant doctors spent over 45 minutes trying to think of any minute changes that might help Karis. Overall the conclusion was to make as few changes as possible. They were disappointed that turning her on her stomach didn't make more of a difference in her oxygen levels. They believe they are dealing with the damage in her lungs from the infection, more so than the infection itself. They expect progress will be very slow and incremental.

(Debbie) My huge concern is for how Karis is handling in her mind and soul all that is happening to her. When she has been in medically-induced comas in the past, she has often suffered horrible nightmares, despite our constant prayers and presence with her. The thought that this might be happening again is unbearable. All I can do is pray, and fill her environment with praise. On her blog, I ask people to pray that her mind and soul will be filled with peace and joy, no matter what is happening to her body.

How I wish I could know what she is experiencing! The ICU docs don't think she is experiencing much at all. They think she is so deeply sedated that we don't have to worry about her mind or soul. But she has come out of deep sedation in the past and told us about nightmares in 3-D. So I don't know, and I worry, and I pray. This is almost all that I can think about.

I play for Karis yet one more peaceful CD about God's love, pray for her once more with one of my daughters, kiss her carefully so I don't bruise her skin, and go home.

This long vigil is getting so very hard. I am so very weary. . .

Day 19, Friday, January 31, 2014

With renewed energy this morning, I decided to go to the hospital by myself so everyone else could have a much-needed break. This was a mistake.

The Infectious Diseases doctor came in and told me she was making an appeal to the FDA for five more days of IV antiviral treatment, because Karis was still "shedding" (duplicating) the virus. The first five days of treatment had not been effective in stopping ongoing damage to Karis' lungs.

The doctor told me that even if the H1N1 had been diagnosed early and treatment started immediately, and even if Karis had been perfectly healthy when she contracted the virus, she would only have had a 50% chance of surviving it. This particular strain of H1N1 has already killed a number of young people this year who had no other health issues. There was an article in the paper about how unusual this was; it wasn't only the very old and the very young who were dying from this flu this year.

Then the doctor told me very gently that even if her appeal were to be granted by the FDA, there might not be time for it to be effective, because Karis's body was shutting down in other ways. Her kidneys, liver, and other organs had largely stopped functioning.

After the doctor left, I forced myself to look objectively at Karis's situation. For the first time, I let myself realize that Karis was going to die. In fact, her body was already dying.

Unless God were to do a spectacular miracle, *Karis was going to die.*

I couldn't grasp it. I couldn't maintain objectivity. I became dizzy and panicky and had to sit down.

I called David and could only say, "I need help." Dave and Rachel arrived as quickly as they could. They took turns being with Karis and staying with me in the waiting room. I couldn't handle going home and being alone, but I couldn't cope with being with Karis, watching her body fall apart while not knowing what was happening in her mind and in her soul.

Day 20, Saturday, February 1, 2014 Karen's Birthday

Our son Dan, back from Mexico, arrived in Pittsburgh late Friday evening, along with a Brazilian friend. Saturday morning the head doctor of the TICU requested a meeting with our family.

Shortly before this meeting, my sister Karen arrived from her home in Hershey, PA. It was Karen's birthday, yet she chose to drive for several hours through winter weather to be with us in this moment.

The TICU doctor explained that everything possible had been done for Karis, and there was nothing more to do. He knew how hard this situation was for us, how much we loved Karis. He and his staff would be available to help us understand her situation as clearly as possible. When we were ready as a family, they would take Karis off of life support. The doctor emphasized that we should take our time, not feel pressured, and give ourselves space for this hugely important moment in our family experience.

Hearing this was hard for all of us, but for our son Dan, who had just arrived and had not walked through the previous days with us, the idea that we were at the end of the line with Karis was too big and painful to absorb. So many times over the years we had heard doctors say that nothing more could be done, and each time Karis came through. What was different this time?

With our family together, Dan suggested that each of us might want to invite a close friend to support us. He called his best friend from DC, who arrived as soon as he could. My sister Karen was there. Rachel had her fiancé Brian. Valerie was profoundly missing her husband Cesar, still in Brazil awaiting his green card and unable to travel until it was granted.

Since so many—especially Dan—wanted to spend time with Karis, I went home. After sharing so much with her for more than thirty years, in this most significant moment of her life I could not be *with her*. I could hardly bear the tension of not knowing what was going on in her mind and heart.

Day 21, Sunday, February 2, 2014

This day God showed me clearly that he was with us and was caring for Karis.

I woke up feeling tremendously burdened for Karis, yet not feeling I could handle being with her. While the family went to the hospital, I stayed home. I was sitting at the kitchen table contemplating breakfast when my cell phone rang. It was my sister Shari, calling from Florida, telling me that in prayer God had told her to say something to me that she didn't fully understand.

The significance of what she told me only makes sense by knowing the bit of history recounted in chapter 19 . Shari said to me, "God asked me to tell you Karis's mind is tucked within his mind. He is holding it for her."

Shari had no idea what these words meant to me. No other message from God could have lifted my burden so completely.

With all my heart I praise you, O God.

Day 22, Monday, February 3, 2014

Last night my eldest sister Linda decided to take a Pittsburgh detour on her way to Guatemala from her home in Iowa. Karen and I picked her up at the airport, and the ICU nurses granted an exception so Linda could see Karis even though visiting hours were over. My heart was at peace as we walked into her room. The enormous burden of concern for her mind and heart that had distressed me for days had been lifted through God's word to me via Shari in Florida.

Still, it was hard to see Karis again with "fresh" eyes, both my own after not being with her for more than 24 hours, and my sister's. The TICU was quiet. Everything was quiet and still, except for the machines still pumping life into Karis' inert body. We talked in hushed tones, respecting the stillness.

One dimension of our experience these days was hard for all of us, but particularly painful for our son Dan. Following the H1N1 diagnosis, our transplant doctor, who cared so well and invested so much in Karis for the past six years, disappeared. We didn't see him again.

Dan felt a profound need to speak with this doctor, to hear from his lips what he thought was happening with Karis. Unaccountably, the doctor refused, even though Dan said over and over to the nurses, "I'm not angry with him. I just need to speak with him." In our most profound crisis, the person we had most depended on seemed to have abandoned us. We could only think that he too was grieving.

At the same time, even though the head doctor of the TICU told us we should not feel rushed to take Karis off the machines, the nurses pressured me to do so. I think this was because they loved Karis and were having a difficult time themselves as they watched her body breaking down.

We agreed as a family to make no decisions about removing life support until all of us were ready. The nurses couldn't understand this. They felt we were willfully prolonging Karis' suffering.

Day 23, Tuesday, February 4, 2014

Blog post by Valerie:

> Our family had a special time with Karis this afternoon, telling her how she was special to us, singing and reading to her. At the end, we each told her that if she was ready to go, she was free – that she should not hang on to life for our sake. She was still deeply sedated. We hoped she could hear us, but we can't be sure.

Dave and I (Debbie) went to bed begging God to take Karis. We could not make the decision to take her off the machines. After fighting for her life since her birth, we could not bear to feel we had taken part in her death.

At the same time, watching the ongoing deterioration of her body systems was becoming unbearable. After our family time with Karis, I moved her leg to make it more comfortable, and her skin split. Even the gentlest touch caused immediate bruising. I had cared intimately for this body for more than thirty years, and now my touch was no longer a blessing; it only did her harm.

I could do nothing more for my precious girl. *Father, take her Home.*

> Keep watch, dear Lord, with those who work, or watch, or weep this night,
> and give your angels charge over those who sleep. Tend the sick, Lord Christ; give rest to the weary, bless the dying, soothe the suffering, pity the afflicted, shield the joyous; and all for your love's sake. Amen.

Day 24, Wednesday, February 5, 2014

Blog post by Valerie:

> This morning the ICU called around 5:15 to tell us Karis's oxygen level was dropping. We all got up and got dressed, but the roads were so icy we could not safely leave home. We were very sorry not to be with Karis in these last moments. We sat in the living room, listening to Bach's Toccata and Fugue, imagining people running to meet Karis in heaven.

> The respiratory therapist told us that she seemed comfortable. She passed at 6:05 am, an hour after her oxygen level started dropping.

> We are grateful that we could say good-bye to her as a family.

> *Our earthly bodies are planted in the ground when we die,*
> *but they will be raised to live forever.*

> *Our bodies are buried in brokenness,*
> *but they will be raised in glory.*

They are buried in weakness,
but they will be raised in strength.

They are buried as natural human bodies,
but they will be raised as spiritual bodies . . .

For our dying bodies must be transformed into bodies that will never die;
our mortal bodies must be transformed into immortal bodies . . .

Thank God! He gives us victory over sin and death through our Lord
Jesus Christ.   (Selected from I Corinthians 15:42-57)

A sword pierced my heart. Yes, it's an apt description. I didn't know such pain was possible. Another transplant mom, who had lost her son, sent me a text: "Just . . . breathe."

I still have that text on my phone.

Karis's Memorial Service, February 15, 2014

Many friends fought blizzard conditions to attend Karis's memorial service at Church of the Ascension in Pittsburgh. Others tried to come and were unable to do so. The entire service can be viewed on YouTube, as can a version with only the music (twenty-two pieces of music!), or with only the talks.

A lovely thing happened at the reception, one of those special touches from God that resonate for weeks and years afterward. Dave and I were talking to people in two separate receiving lines, because so many kind people wanted to express to us their love for Karis. When it was her turn, our friend Janet grabbed my arm and said "Debbie, I just have to know—who is Michael?"

Caught off guard, I said "Well, we had a son we named Michael, but I miscarried him."

Janet breathed a huge sigh and said, "Oh, I'm so glad to know I'm not crazy!"

The story was this: Tuesday night before Karis died, Janet was not able to sleep, feeling she needed to intercede for Karis. Every time she closed her eyes, Janet "saw" Karis in the ICU. Three large, stately angels watched over her from three corners of the bed. (Later, reading Karis's journal, I learned she had seen them while she was still on the floor, and named them Hope, Faith, and Love.)

What confused Janet was a fourth angel, a little one, who spent the night playing on Karis's bed, running back and forth, jumping up and down, whispering in Karis's ear and giggling. . . . "Lord," Janet pleaded. "Please tell me who that little angel is and what on earth he is doing there!"

Finally, Janet heard the Lord say, "Oh, that's just Michael. He wanted to help bring Karis Home, so we figured the easiest way was to send him as an angel."

That was all the explanation Janet received.

At 6:05 the next morning, Janet watched the three angels, and Michael, escort Karis from her bed in the ICU, leaving only her body. Then Janet fell asleep.

Since she had no idea who Michael was, Janet had wondered ever since whether she had made up the whole thing, vivid as it seemed to her.

How precious of the Lord, while taking Karis from us, to give us this glimpse of our son Michael Derek. We lost him without ever knowing him, on January 22, 1987. It had been surreal for me to lie in my hospital bed grieving while down the hall babies of the same gestational age as Michael were being killed on purpose and outside, protestors were chanting and marching around the hospital. At his memorial service, a woman shared with us a clear vision of Michael in Heaven helping care for and heal the babies who arrived there through abortion. I now imagine Karis helping Michael in this work.

This glimpse of our son through Janet let us know that he is playful and mischievous, as full of life and joy as his big sister. From the start, Karis has had her little brother Michael to introduce her to how things are done in Heaven!

In the years since Karis died, there have been Karis sightings, related to me by people whose vision I trust. One of them is particularly poignant for our family. Rachel had invited Karis to be a bridesmaid at her wedding, September 6, 2014, seven months after Karis's death. Grieving over Karis's absence at this milestone event in their lives, Rachel and Brian decided to honor Karis with a moment of silence at the beginning of the ceremony.

Our pastor and his wife from Brazil, Vandeir and Hildete, were present at the wedding. With her limited English, when suddenly everything stopped and the sanctuary was quiet, Hildete didn't understand what was happening. She looked around, trying to figure it out, and saw Karis dance down the aisle and take her place with the other bridesmaids. Karis was radiant with joy. Hildete was all goosebumps when she learned later what that moment of quiet had been about. Only after Rachel and Brian's honeymoon was Hildete able to tell Rachel that Karis *was* present at her wedding after all!

Karis as we imagine her now

CHAPTER 21

All I See Is Grace

How would Karis tell her own story?

This question has been in my mind through all the hours I've spent reading, weeping, and laughing my way through her journals, sifting through years of memories and uncounted discoveries within the thousands of pages of her small, closely-written script.

I believe Karis would say God was faithful. He was faithful to her personally and to his word to her through friends' prayers when she was 16. I believe she would say the two rails, the Promise and the Prophecy, carried her roller coaster safely through darkness and light into the arms of Jesus.

The Promise: *"Seu amado está guardado"* (Your beloved is set apart). In her last weeks of life, Karis reached the insight that her lifelong interpretation of the promise might not be correct. She had thought it meant she would marry and support a special man in his ministry in the Kingdom. She realized that the Portuguese could instead be interpreted as "Your beloved is protected," or saved, or covered.

God's direction of Karis in 2008 to pray daily for Anthony and his family had seemed unreasonable, as she was trying to "get over" her love for him. Now she saw that her obedience could have been used by God to support and protect this beloved one—that Anthony indeed was her Amado. Indeed, Karis had prayed for her Amado ever since she received this promise when she was sixteen. She saw that her twelve years of loving Anthony could be compared to the holy love of Clare for Francis.[24]

---

[24] Karis grew up hearing stories about Francis and Clare from her dad. Dave has been drawn to St. Francis since before we married. If you're not familiar with Francis' story or Clare's, he recommends *The Journey and the Dream* by Murray Bodo as the best of the many books he's read about Francis. You can Google movies about Francis, the most famous being "Brother Sun, Sister Moon." Francis and Clare deeply loved and supported each other. At the same time, once she was cloistered, they only met twice. His was a traveling missionary calling; hers was a cloistered intercessory calling—very much like Anthony and Karis.

Really? That was my skeptical thought when I first read these ideas in some of Karis's very last journal entries. Was this just her way of rationalizing a huge disappointment in her life, the fact that she never married and never had the daughter she dreamed about?

Admittedly, my skepticism was linked to my disappointment with Anthony in the way he had treated Karis in the breakup of their dating relationship. Karis worked this through with him and came to peace. I had not. I had relegated Anthony to a part of Karis's past that was best forgotten.

Until I read the journals, I was not aware that Karis had continued to feel deeply bonded to Anthony even after the conversation in 2007 that resolved so much of her anguish over their friendship. I didn't know she prayed for him and his family every day after his brother's wedding in 2008, the last time she saw him. I wasn't privy to her ongoing communication with him both by email and by phone. I imagine Karis didn't discuss any of this with me at least in part because she knew I had not resolved my feelings about Anthony.

In light of what I learned from Karis's journals, and continuing to ask the question, "How would Karis tell her own story?" I decided to contact Anthony to learn whether he had anything to say in regard to Karis's ideas. I was fully prepared for him to mirror my own thoughts, that his story with Karis had ended long before and had no further relevance to his life.

Anthony's response surprised me in many ways: his candor, his clear ongoing care for Karis, his courtesy in expressing to me his sorrow over the suffering he had caused her, and the role he as a Franciscan feels she still plays in his life through her ongoing prayers for him. He told me, "I get the sense that I am, still now to this day, supported, sustained, and loved by Karis and her prayers."

Anthony has dedicated his life to service of God and his Body. He feels called to work in a part of the world most of us would consider dangerous, where others have died as martyrs. His belief that Karis intercedes for him in the very presence of God encourages him in the daily challenges of his ministry. I believe Karis would say with great joy that the "Amado" promise was fulfilled, in ways she neither anticipated nor understood until close to the end of her life on earth. We will understand this mystery clearly only in Heaven.

The Prophecy: *"You will be a door; through you many nations will see Christ. You will be given a key."* In her journals, Karis does not express understanding that this was fulfilled through her life. She had imagined it meant she would have a large international ministry for the Lord. With that in mind, she wondered whether she had failed God in some way.

When I read this, though, a dozen images swept through my mind of Karis loving and comforting and praying with people from many nations gathered in hospital waiting rooms or intensive care units, most frequently Arabic speakers from countries closed to North Americans. Not once to my knowledge did a husband or brother or father refuse to allow Karis to read Biblical Scriptures in Arabic or pray with one of her friends, in the hospital or out.

I don't know how many Arabic Bibles were taken back with these friends to their countries, in honor perhaps of their friendship with Karis, but perhaps with deeper intent. Most of Karis's Arabic-speaking friends were surprised to learn that the Bible existed in Arabic long before it was translated into English in 1526 AD. The earliest intact fragment in Arabic is from the eighth century, but Arabic Bibles are referred to from the earliest Christian churches in Syria and Egypt.

My first thought was that the "key" in the prophecy might be Karis's five languages: English, Portuguese, Spanish, French, and Arabic. With them she could speak to the heart of virtually everyone who came to Pittsburgh for intestinal transplant.

Another key, however, was the very fact that she was there, in that space, also a patient, with the same IV pole and hospital garb they wore; facing the same transplants, treatments, indignities, complications, and suffering. *Knowing* it all from the inside out; knowing and sharing the Source of hope and strength and joy and love, Karis's life spoke vividly of Incarnation.

Karis's mind increasingly betrayed her as kidney failure took its toll, making communication with all these friends more difficult. Shortly before this time, the Egyptian doctor who had attracted these patients to Pittsburgh from across the Arabic-speaking world, transferred to a different hospital in a different city, and took most of his patients with him.

Thus the window of time when these people were gathered in Pittsburgh was the window in which Karis was there too, actively loving them, serving them, and blessing them with God's Word and prayer. Surely, in this sense, Karis's need for intestinal transplant, and our coming to Pittsburgh was part of the "key" that opened the door for people from many nations to see Christ.

Anthony wrote to me that he feels Karis's ministry "is not finished; it is just beginning." He described several times when his telling of her story (and their story) built bridges to young people. Anthony says,

> Her testimony, and maybe my testimony regarding her, may be something that God wants to use to speak to people about His love and the power of His forgiveness . . . I don't think I am romanticizing things. I think I am just looking at what God actually did in her life, and how I think her testimony will continue to touch people . . . Through her I have had my most complete experience of my own fragility and of being loved and forgiven. This makes all the difference as I proclaim God's forgiveness and offer it to others.

If Karis were telling her story, I believe she would say that like a surgeon, God wounds, but he also heals. She would say there is joy at the heart of the universe. She would say, flashing her brilliant smile, "Aren't they beautiful?" about each person God created. She would say "I love you," to God, to me, and to you.

After reading her journals, I believe Karis would say that she was broken over the feet of the Body of Christ so that the perfume of her intercessions for the healing of the Body could rise up to God. And that matters more than the many ambitious plans she had for her life.

I think she would want to say to you, "All that stuff you're going through right now—I think I kind of get it. But more importantly, Jesus totally gets it. And he loves and cares far more than you can imagine. Climb into his lap and let him carry it for you."

She would say, "God's grace was sufficient for me. His power was made perfect in my weakness."

She would say, "I always knew God would keep me on earth exactly as long as he had use for me there."

She would say, "The strength of the Lord was my joy. The joy of the Lord was my strength."

I think she would say, steepling her fingers and rubbing her thumbs together, her eyes bright with glee, *"You have NO IDEA what's waiting for you here with Michael and me!"*

I think she would say to me, "Mama, be at peace. You did what you could" (Mark 14:8).

I believe she would say she has forgotten the pain; that indeed our present troubles are small and don't last very long, yet they produce glory that vastly outweighs them and will last forever (2 Corinthians 4:17).

She would say, *"All I see is grace."*

Dave and Karis on the white sand dunes of Natal, Brazil

Reflections by Dave on the Fourth Anniversary of Karis's Death

February 5, 2018

Karis…

Lord, who am I and who is Debbie to have such an extraordinary daughter? To me, her life seemed sacramental. That is well expressed in Deb's choice of book title "All I See Is Grace."

Words that come to mind when I think of Karis: her love, smile, beauty, mind, passion, support, suffering and glory.

1. Love. Karis loved God above all else and lived in his love. In her forced confinements she turned even more deeply to him. Her prayer life was extraordinary.

    Karis's love and relational grace was evident in her indiscriminant giving of herself to one and all: street children and upper class; Brazilian and American; Protestant and Catholic; Muslim and Hindu. She involved herself with so many at Notre Dame despite her tremendous physical difficulties. And in a very personal sense, she loved me. I failed so much as a husband and father. She chose not to dwell on my shortcomings and instead affirmed and celebrated who I am. She deeply accepted and valued me.

2. Smile. Lighting her whole face with radiance. Her smile came from deep within her. She seemed to be deeply integrated, smiling from her soul. Her eyes lit up. She appreciated and valued and embraced whatever she was smiling at: art, creation, beauty or a person or people. She saw God everywhere, I think. Even lying in bed with little ability to do much, her face would usually light up if I came to her for any reason. God smiled on her and through her to the rest of us.

3. Beauty. Karis was physically beautiful, her physical grace expressed especially in dance. As her illness gradually robbed her of physical abilities, her inner beauty continued to shine. She was attractive from the inside out and attracted people from every walk of life.

Karis radiated the love of Christ and the beauty of Christ. I'm reminded of the old chorus "Let the beauty of Jesus be seen in me; all his wonderful passion and purity! O Thou, Spirit divine, all my nature refine, 'til the beauty of Jesus be seen in me." Karis's Mary in her booklet *Mary's Diary* seems to me to reflect Karis's own character. As Gabriel says to Mary (in The Message, Luke 1.28):

Good morning!
You're beautiful with God's beauty,
Beautiful inside and out!

That was Karis. That is Karis!

4. Mind. Karis had a very high IQ. She was brilliant. She became fascinated with whatever mattered to someone who was important to her. She read and digested textbooks on economics or law or whatever because she wanted to understand and interact profitably with friends interested in those topics. Her poetry was perhaps the greatest expression of her mind. Yet she never let anyone feel inferior or lesser.

Perhaps Karis's greatest fear and trial was losing her brilliant mind. While she wept over that and truly grieved her loss, she did not let it define her. She was still Karis, even though a modified version of what she had been. She made the painful adjustments she had to make and kept on loving and enjoying life as God allowed. Undoubtedly, one of her greatest blessings was the repeated prophetic message that God was protecting her mind within His own mind. That upheld her in her worst moments.

5. Passion. Karis was passionately alive. She embraced life and whomever or whatever was immediately in front of her. She was perhaps the most truly multi-cultural person I've known. Yet one wasn't struck by her, as much as by feeling valued and understood. She was passionate about God, about her studies, about Anthony, about her writing and poetry, about dance. She refused to allow

herself to be defined as an invalid. Even if it meant courting death, she was going to *live*.

Karis's passion brought others alive, including me. More than anyone else she was passionate about my calling and ministry, firmly committed to God's call and direction for my life.

6. Support. Karis was a servant to one and all. She gladly served and gave herself to American football players at Notre Dame, the Indians, Brazilians, Latins, Africans, Asians, and Muslims, fellow honors students, the dancers, the Gospel choir, her professors, her nurses, WOG and Iron Sharpens Iron, People of Praise, the Catholic worship services and every group she encountered.

Karis supported me. She wanted me to freely and deeply give myself to my calling even though it meant being far from her. She rejoiced in being with me, but she truly sent me back out with a full and happy heart each time I left her.

Karis's support of others was especially expressed in her active intercession for them. She was a contemplative. She was also an extrovert. And so she took many people very deeply to God in prayer. How blessed I am to have been one of them; blessed in believing I still am one of them as she intercedes for me from heaven.

7. Suffering. I don't personally know anyone who has suffered physically more than Karis. Like Jesus, she didn't let suffering or pain define her or become a barrier between her and God or her and others. She somehow overrode it to the point that few people knew her constant battle. She let it refine and purify her, and only shone more as a result. She identified incredibly deeply with others because she connected with their inner lives and their pain. When forced into hospitals or her sickbed she made a bridge of her illness and pain to others whom God brought to her there.

8. Glory. When I commented on beauty above, I was overlapping with glory. God's glory was magnified in her through her suffering. Karis embraced 2 Corinthians particularly – her light and temporary suffering not comparable to the weight of glory God was giving her; her weaknesses just doors and windows for God's strength and grace to be revealed. She gloried in being God's beloved daughter, even with all her physical handicaps. She gloried in the Scriptures and learning and growing and knowing. God's character shone through her. To know her was to know a little more of her Father.

Because Karis was often in pain and limited by her illness, she focused more than most people on God. She drew people to him, to life, to light, to delight, to joy.

Thank you, Lord, for the precious gift of being Karis's dad. I'm the only person who ever experienced that and I'm incredibly grateful. She only ever had two parents and I'm one of them and I'm married to the other! She needed a great deal from us, taken mostly from Debbie. But she gave as much or more as she took. She took what she had to; she gave what she could. Deb and I are far richer because of her, far better people, far more Christ-like. We understand hope much more tangibly because of her. Grace. Love. Faith. Your sovereignty. Your glory.

Thank you for sharing Karis with us for 30 years. Thank you that she is tucked into you and that very shortly we will be enjoying her again. Thank you for our belief that she continues to look out for us and accompany us in some fashion. Thank you that she is free from all pain and fully herself, more fully than any of us can imagine. All we see is Grace, past, present and future. Deb and I are very grateful for the gift of Karis, a visible sign of your invisible grace, our own personal sacrament.

Rachel and Karis: Fun at Frick Park

Finding Grace Even in Death

By Rachel Kornfield Becker

Is there ever grace in death? My experience says yes. When a loved one's suffering seems interminable there is relief related to the fact that they are no longer in pain, and no longer subject to relentless medical indignities.

The first time I felt that Karis might actually die (not the first time she was at risk but the first time it came home to me that this might really happen) was in 2004 when I was nineteen years old. Karis was about to lose her first transplant, in an "impossible" surgery given that she was in a coma on a ventilator with severe pneumonia and a disintegrating intestine. In the surgery waiting room Mom turned to me with strain in every line of her face and said, "What kind of flowers do you think Karis would like at her memorial service?"

I was shocked into a stumbling senseless reply – not only had it never occurred to me to wonder what Karis's favorite flowers were, I couldn't quite get my head around the idea that my mom was taking this question seriously. My mom the ever-hopeful, the ever-resilient was talking about the death of my sister – the miracle baby who against all odds ALWAYS survived! I mostly responded with an internal sense of "whaaaaaaaat?" I didn't realize this at the time but most of me believed that sitting in that waiting room was just part of the process of waiting for the next miracle.

I wonder sometimes what my grief process would have been like if Karis had died then. I know I had fewer emotional, spiritual, social and experiential resources with which to deal with it. I mostly imagine I would have fallen into an abyss and taken years to come out. I had no context for death, no sense of light in the darkness of that possibility.

In comparison, the actual timing of Karis' death came to me as grace. Sometimes I feel guilty about this – after all, she went through so much in the 10 intervening years. But in some ways I believe Karis would have me receive those years as a gift from her. She fought so hard to be there for her Beloveds. She fought so hard for the joy of life. I am reminded of one scene in her last year or two, her body already significantly compromised, when she sat in a wheelchair at church with her hands weaving graceful shapes in the air. If she couldn't dance to the worship with her whole body, she was sure going to do so at least with her hands!

Between 2004 and 2014 several things happened that caused the timing of Karis' death to come across to me as grace. I weathered (with help and support from my family) several severe mental health crises and came to a place of stability more solid than my pre-crises world. I gained a clear sense of future that neither college nor my first stumbling post-college years had provided for me. I developed a strong and positive lasting relationship with a mental health therapist. I started grad school in social work to become a mental health clinician myself, a field I was truly passionate about.

I started an internship at Pittsburgh Pastoral Institute, a place that would comfort me and shepherd me in my grief. I met Lisa, who became my roommate during grad school and the years beforehand, a beautiful, resilient woman who knows how to get through tough things. I met Brian, who would become my husband – a tender, caring, deeply listening man who held me and heard me as I cried countless times both before and after Karis's death and wasn't scared away by my grief and confusion. We got engaged in November 2013, not knowing Karis would die less than three months later. Added to rich and good community, I received this grace: the concept of death stopped feeling so foreign to me.

It turned out we had some warning that Karis's death was near because her kidneys started failing. It was oddly gentle in that there was no immediate crisis. We were so used to jumping from crisis to crisis that the doctor's prognosis was a surprising change in pattern: Karis was likely to die within a year, not from some medical anomaly but from kidney failure, well known and prosaic. My brother and I went for a walk the next time he visited Pittsburgh, around and around the neighborhood, both trying to grapple with the idea that this time Karis's death was very likely to be real... maybe? It was still hard to believe. My mom researched and discarded every possible life-saving intervention ... multiple times. I gradually began to get accustomed to the idea that we might lose my sister.

Surprisingly, one thing that helped me was an actual academic class on grief and loss. The professor knew her stuff. She also completely freaked the class out at the beginning by telling us that every semester she teaches the class someone in it experiences a death. This time she was wrong – she was off by two months.

Professor Amy DeGurian had worked in hospice and learned to walk bravely into the reality of grief and loss. She taught me that death could be gentle, even peaceful, when family members and the dying person accept the process and use remaining time to strengthen relationships: apologize where needed, make amends where possible, be present to one another. She had us read books by people describing their own experiences of death and grief. She augmented Kubler-Ross' stages of grief with J. William Worden's Four Tasks of Grief – a more active way to think about the flow of grief. Altogether, the message I took away was that although death is terrible, it is also natural. It is easier when we face into it instead of running away from it. There are choices that can be made in most cases about what someone's end-of-life looks like. Hospice provides some amazing options.

Also, grief never looks the same for two different people. Every family struggles with this after death because they grieve differently and easily misunderstand each other's responses as grief ebbs and flows. A grieving person draws close and then away and close and away. Frequently one family member is in the process of drawing close while another needs to pull away. Tensions arise because different family members legitimately need opposite things. When my own family experienced these dynamics it was harder than I expected it to be. But having a framework for understanding was helpful.

I also learned that grief comes in waves, even unexpected ones years afterward around anniversaries or birthdays or randomly when something triggers a memory of the person. Although grief generally eases over time, there's no "right" timetable – it varies for every person and situation. The expectation that anyone will ever "get over it" is a complete misunderstanding. Instead, we adjust to a "new normal." My brother said a year or so ago, "Losing Karis was like losing my right arm. But I'm learning to live with only one arm." There is grace in this: we don't truly want to forget our loved ones; we want them to continue with us. They are part of us even after death.

In so many ways I had already turned toward the acceptance of Karis's death before she died. In those last couple of years I could not look at her and wish long life for her – not in that state of struggle and suffering, especially not after her bright and active mind started going. I could see the inescapable reality of her failing body.

Despite all of this preparation, though, the three to four days before Karis's death were some of the worst in my life. What made it so was being asked to pull the plug in the ICU when the doctors thought there was no more hope. The tension over this between family members and my sense that Karis possibly suffered psychologically while we dithered made those days nearly unbearable.

Finally, I suggested to the family that we have a time of saying good-bye. (Thank you, Professor DeGurian, for teaching me about the importance of ritual!) It was poignant, it was beautiful, it was necessary, it was rich. The music we listened to together still resounds in my soul. At the end we stood in silence, surrounding a body that was literally coming apart. It came to me to say aloud to Karis that she was free to go. To my surprise, each one in the family repeated a similar sentiment in their own way. A few hours later, she went. As a result of that experience and many stories I have heard from other people since then, I have come to believe very deeply in the power of a family to release a loved one to a peaceful death when the time comes. After fighting *for* Karis's life for over thirty years, it was a grace that we didn't have to pull the plug. I think that made the grief process easier for all of us.

Still, the first few weeks after Karis's death were agony. One of the foundations had dropped out of my world. She was my older sister and I had never known life without her in it. My family faced a major lifestyle and relational change, because so much had necessarily been centered on taking care of Karis. None of us yet knew how we were going to weather that—we didn't know who we were without her. In some ways we're still figuring it out, although sometime in the first year I became certain our sense of family was going to survive intact.

One of the graces in those first weeks is what I call the parade of aunts. My mom has five sisters and most of them came to be with us from all over the country and the world, one after the other. I had never experienced so much support from my mom's family. Uncles, cousins and friends also contributed, working together with us and the clergy of our church to make Karis's memorial service truly beautiful. I've never been to another one like it. Among other things we had a flower screen. Each person who entered could pick up a flower and come to the front of the church to weave it into the screen. It was a beautiful picture of the way Karis wove together her Beloveds against the framework of her life. It also imaged the loveliness of each friend's enrichment of her experience. The music and the reminiscences and the homily were true tributes; out-pourings of grace.

Meanwhile, the dean and professors at my School of Social Work were gracious around my sudden inability to function academically. For about six weeks in the middle of what was supposed to be my last semester I just couldn't do it. They worked with me to adjust my class schedule as necessary and in the end I graduated in August instead of May. I am so grateful for their understanding and flexibility.

Six months after Karis died, in September 2014, Brian and I got married. Though the year had been shadowed by grief, my memories of our wedding are surprisingly joyous. I felt overwhelmed by goodness. We remembered Karis through a moment of silence at the beginning of the ceremony and then focused on wedding-ing with a congregation full of many of the same people who had been at the memorial service. What a blessing!

About a year after Karis's death (Jan/Feb 2015), I noticed a gradual movement: her loss was no longer the central core of my emotional world. My grief was sinking appropriately into the foundations, leaving me space and energy to look toward the future. That summer Brian and I bought a house together and settled into a fulfilling, contented, grace-filled routine as we moved deeper into life and work together.

Over the second year after Karis's death (Feb 2015 to Feb 2016) my memories of her increasingly shifted toward joyful instead of painful. I began to have an image of a wholly well Karis, dancing in heaven and sometimes giving me her mischievous, animated smile when I tasted a new adventure.

In the fourth year, my sister Valerie and her husband Cesar had a baby, Caleb Elliott, the first of the new generation of our family. And now in spring 2018 as the world buds around me I am reminded that new life always returns to us after death.

Rereading this book now has brought up a lot for me again – the hard parts that I had allowed to sink away. Grief comes in waves. But those hard parts have become part of the texture of my life that I hold dear and would not change. I am who I am because of them; they shape the way I do my work. So I will be me and honor the part of Karis that is in me and enjoy her quirky smile when I embark on a new adventure. If she could give us a message today, I think it would be this: "Live free! Don't let yourself be held down by the pain. Pain passes. Joy is forever." There is pain mixed with the grace, but I will not for that reason refuse the grace. It is beautiful.

Thanks

"To begin," my brother Dan advised, "write down everything you can think of about Karis. Then you'll know what you have to work with in shaping a book." That effort, combined with what I pulled from Karis's journals (conservatively, I thought), resulted in an initial manuscript of about 900,000 words. That would have been a book of over 3200 pages!

So I started working with the enormous mound of clay I had on the table, pulling out stones and grass and roots and some of the debris of my own emotional processing. I kneaded and pounded to release air bubbles and make the clay more malleable. I walked around and around the worktable considering how to shape the clay. I felt overwhelmed, because with all of this effort I only managed to reduce the volume by half, and I felt stuck.

Then Anthony wrote, "This is a God story. It needs to be told as fully as possible." Don't give up, is the message I heard. "Fully as possible" meant it had to be brief enough to be accessible. But how?

One morning I woke up thinking, "My family is full of writers! What if I ask them to help?!" The result of this crazy idea was a team of twelve family and friends who each took a section of the 400,000 word manuscript and gave me suggestions about how to shape their piece of it. My sister Linda read through the entire 400,000 word mess and then the 200,000 words that resulted from this intensive effort, to bring some coherence and continuity to the molding of so many potters.

But it was still way too big. I let it settle for a while, then went back to work myself, cutting mercilessly (I thought) to 125,000. "Nope, way too long," my friend Gerry, author of twenty books, told me. "You'll never be able to sell that; no one will read it. Aim for 60,000. 50,000 would be even better. People just don't read books these days. This will be the hardest thing you've ever done—you'll feel like you're cutting out your soul—but you have to do it."

I didn't make 60,000, much less 50. Indeed, when I look at the result my soul bleeds. I feel I have done Karis an injustice, representing her life with what is here. But some of the stories and journal treasures will make their way into other formats: Karis's stories and poetry, my blog "But God," perhaps some writing about the impact of chronic illness on a family and about survival when life lacerates your sense of yourself. The clay is still there, and can be molded into more pots than just this one.

My husband Dave steadfastly believed in *All I See Is Grace,* and gave me a six-month "sabbatical" from our mission work to help the clay find its shape. After the manuscript was with an agent for six months and I was ready to give up, his steady faith pulled me through a crisis of my own doubts.

So when I look at the cover and see "by Debra Kornfield," *I* know, and now you do too, that all of these people, and others who gave me feedback along the way, should also have their names on the cover.

You know who you are. I thank you.

About the Author

The fourth of eight children of missionaries to a remote village of Guatemala, Debra Kornfield faced profound "city shock" when she moved with her husband David and four small children to the megalopolis of São Paulo, Brazil in 1990. This was her home for fourteen years until she moved to Pittsburgh in 2004 to support their daughter Karis through intestinal transplant, never dreaming that over the next fourteen years, Pittsburgh would become home.

Debra is a nurse with a graduate degree in family counseling. She published three books in Brazil, one of them a groundbreaking book on care for survivors of childhood sexual abuse. She loves hiking, playing with her grandson, cultivating Karis's Friendship Garden, teaching Scripture and counseling in three languages, writing, and traveling with Dave to the ten Latin American countries where they now work. She enjoys writing for and reading the stories people send for her blog, https://ButGod.blog, and is delighted that biweekly chats keep her in touch with her seven siblings.

Debra met her husband Dave as a freshman at Wheaton College, where she earned a B.A. in English Literature. Dave helped put her through Rush University, where she received her B.S. in Nursing the same month he was awarded his Ph.D. from the University of Chicago. In 1988, two weeks before their fourth child was born, David and Debra joined One Challenge International. They live in Pittsburgh, but travel frequently to Latin America and West Africa for their mission work with OCI.